REBUILDING OUR SCHOOLS FROM THE BOTTOM UP

The aim of this book is to explore how teachers, students and parents can be given more of a say in the education system – in how schools are organised, and in what and how children learn. The book does not promote a specific view of education, but considers the means by which educational purposes and approaches can be conceived, agreed and enacted democratically – a precursor to a flourishing democratic society.

   Rebuilding Our Schools from the Bottom Up has been written in response to significant changes which have taken place in the education system over the past 30 years. In England at least, these changes have resulted in an increasingly centralised system in which the voices of those who teach, those who learn, and those whose children go to school have been marginalised.

The book covers four main areas:

- **Teacher voice:** listening to the professionals
- **Student voice:** involving students as active participants in their education
- **Parent voice:** building a genuine home–school partnership
- **School community voice:** developing a shared vision

With inspiring examples from around the UK and overseas and a range of resources that can be used by senior leaders, teachers and parents, the book aims to encourage and support transformative change so that schools can meet the needs of the communities they exist to serve.

Fiona Carnie is an educationalist, parent and writer. She has been involved in encouraging and supporting new initiatives in the alternative and state sectors for many years and has written widely about the need for new educational approaches.

REBUILDING OUR SCHOOLS FROM THE BOTTOM UP

Listening to Teachers, Children and Parents

Fiona Carnie

Routledge
Taylor & Francis Group

LONDON AND NEW YORK

First published 2018
by Routledge
2 Park Square, Milton Park, Abingdon, Oxon OX14 4RN

and by Routledge
711 Third Avenue, New York, NY 10017

Routledge is an imprint of the Taylor & Francis Group, an informa business

© 2018 Fiona Carnie

British Library Cataloguing in Publication Data
A catalogue record for this book is available from the British Library

Library of Congress Cataloging in Publication Data
A catalog record for this book has been requested

ISBN: 978-1-138-21186-5 (hbk)
ISBN: 978-1-138-21188-9 (pbk)
ISBN: 978-1-315-45189-3 (ebk)

Typeset in Interstate
by Out of House Publishing

For my parents

CONTENTS

FIGURES

ACKNOWLEDGEMENTS

This book's journey has been long in the making and I have learned from many people en route.

The journey started with my work at Human Scale Education – an education reform movement founded to promote "education as if people matter". I would like to acknowledge the enormous influence of Satish Kumar, Mike Davies, Martin and Laura Diamond, Colin Hodgetts, Mildred Masheder, Mary Tasker, John Thomson and Philip Toogood. To begin my career in education working alongside people who were so clear in their vision and values was a great privilege.

For a number of years I worked with Michael Fielding, first at the University of Sussex and then at the Institute of Education, on a range of projects focusing on the importance of voice and participation in educational transformation. The humanity and person-centred values which are at the core of all of Michael's work have inspired many, not least me. He has done an incredible job in helping to keep alive the work of educators from past generations – notably John Dewey, John Macmurray, Loris Malaguzzi and Alex Bloom – from whom there is so much to learn.

I spent five years working at the RSA Academy in the West Midlands – a new school that was set up to rethink secondary education in order to transform learning and lives in an area of significant deprivation. I am grateful to the then principal, Mick Gernon, who was fearless in his drive to improve outcomes for children growing up in challenging circumstances. He gave me considerable freedom and support to try out new ideas to engage our students, our parents, our staff and our community. My colleagues there, in particular Daulton Redmond, the current principal, Sally Weale, Lesley James, Mat Carpenter, Arvind Batra and Racheal Baker, were a fantastic team to work with. I am still in awe of the commitment and sheer hard work that they all put in for the benefit of students. Our work together has certainly informed my thinking.

Since the early 1990s I have been involved in different capacities with the European Forum for Freedom in Education (EFFE), an organisation that was set up initially to support the liberalisation of education systems in eastern European countries after the fall of the Berlin Wall. I have made friends and colleagues across Europe through whom I have been introduced to many exciting schools and initiatives. In particular, I would like to pay tribute to the work of Ole Pederson (Denmark), Dirk Höfflich, Lilian Jüchtern and Ingo Krampen (Germany), Anne Charrière (France), Eva Becker (Austria) and Kaisa Lange (Finland).

I have learned so much from all these colleagues in terms of how education might be different.

And now to this book: my thanks first of all to my editor at Routledge, Helen Pritt, for her support and also to Clare Ashworth for commissioning the work.

The book is full of inspiring projects and schools around the UK and further afield and I am indebted to the many contributors who have written about their experiences. They are all practitioners who, in one way or another, are working incredibly hard to walk the talk and it is humbling that they were all prepared to give their time to contribute. Through the various case studies they have brought the book alive and demonstrated that listening to people and trusting them really works.

I am grateful to Esme Bristow for her feedback. I would also like to thank Ian Cunningham and Graham Leicester for their contributions and for generously allowing me to use resources that they have developed.

My family, as always, has given me huge support. Jamie Carnie and Indigo Carnie both read and commented on various drafts. Their feedback has been invaluable and without doubt has made it a better book. Any errors are, of course, my own.

Finally, I would like to express my ongoing gratitude to Mary Tasker with whom I have worked over many years. There seems to be no end to her support, her encouragement and her wisdom. As always, she has been a sounding board and critical friend in this project and I appreciate it deeply.

Introduction

This is a book about democracy. It is about strengthening schools by making them more democratic and in turn, strengthening democracy through schools, thus contributing to the development of a democratic society. It is envisaged as a book of hope – the hope that by placing democracy at the centre of the education process, schools can play their rightful role in fostering democratic citizens. And through collaborative decision-making, schools will be better able to meet the needs of the communities they exist to serve.

As John Dewey, one of the most influential education reformers of the twentieth century, argued in 1916:

> the only form of society which facilitates the continued evolution of the human species is a democratic form of society, and furthermore, the development of such a democratic society is dependent to a large degree on the democratisation of schools and schooling.

And yet, 100 years later, democracy is largely absent from the English education system. School students have little chance to contribute to decisions about what they are going to learn and how they are going to learn it; parents are not routinely involved in school decision-making; and the majority of teachers have little say in what and how they teach nor are they able to contribute to discussions about the direction of their school. The purpose of the book is to address that deficit.

The unravelling of local authorities has been a major force in the erosion of democracy. Their role in planning, supporting and monitoring local schools has been diminished. With more and more schools becoming academies, any sense of local accountability has almost entirely gone. Over the last few decades power has been transferred to the Secretary of State for Education so that the government's agenda can be imposed from above. The last three Secretaries of State for Education have had no background in education and the policies they have doggedly introduced, in the face of much opposition from the profession, have been politically driven.

Underlying these government-imposed changes is the neo-liberal agenda which is threatening other public services such as the NHS. Just as our health services are increasingly being delivered by private companies, so too is education. Through the academisation and free school programme – over 50 per cent of secondary schools are now part of an academy chain – the government is systematically transferring our schools into private hands. Yet there is no robust evidence to show that academies achieve better results for their young people than do schools under local authority control. The National Foundation for Educational Research (NFER) published a report in 2015 which stated that "attainment progress in sponsored academies compared to non-academy schools is not significantly different over time when the outcomes are measured as GCSE points". Furthermore, a report into the results of multi-academy trusts from the Chief Inspector of Schools in March 2016 found that only one in seven of these chains showed improved outcomes for its students. In spite of this, the current government is committed to turning all our schools into academies. This is about shrinking the state and allowing market forces into education.

By emphasising competition, schools are set against each other through the league tables. The "best" schools can expand and increase their market share; those less successful go to the wall. And the less successful schools are usually those in areas of hardship and deprivation. In spite of the dangers of the privatisation model as exposed by former US Assistant Secretary of Education, Diane Ravitch, in her book *Reign of Error* (2013), England is following the American model lock, stock and barrel.

It is a divisive agenda, one which is creating social inequity. Compelling schools to focus on targets and testing so that they do well in the league tables causes children, parents and teachers undue stress. Many teachers are leaving the profession as they feel unable to go along with this mechanistic approach. Numerous headship positions are vacant. And many parents are confused. They have been sold a narrow view of education which enables them to compare schools and select what they feel to be the best for their child, only to find, in many cases, that they cannot get their child into the school of their choice.

But there is another way. Whilst educators in other European countries – and beyond – complain that they are being forced to follow the Anglo-American example, closer to home the governments of Scotland and Wales are forging a different path. Neither country is going down the privatisation route and both Wales and Scotland are defining their own approaches to curriculum development and assessment. In both countries, local authorities play a key role in supporting local schools and holding them to account. There is still a connection between communities, schools and local government, which whilst imperfect, serves to strengthen rather than undermine democracy. The devolved governments of both nations understand the importance of working in partnership with young people, with parents and with local communities and look to build on those part-nerships rather than emasculate them.

At the time of writing there are some small signs of hope in England. The rigor-ous application of market principles to schools may change as Ofsted softens its approach to testing and the curriculum under its new Chief Inspector. And some politicians are beginning to question the merits of neo-liberalism per se. Amidst these tentative signs of change, now is the time to strengthen our public institu-tions through active engagement.

The purpose of this book is thus to explore how schools can become more democratic: to ask how they can protect themselves from the unreasonable demands of a politically motivated agenda, counter the incursions of the corpo-rate world and better meet the needs of the communities they exist to serve. It is about how the voices of teachers, students and parents can be strengthened.

It aims to be a practical book borne out of an inhospitable political climate. It offers a radical, bottom-up solution to a far-reaching top-down agenda. It chal-lenges us all to be citizens and to take joint responsibility for our public institu-tions – in this case – our schools. It argues for action rather than passivity in the interests of creating an education system capable of shaping a diverse, tolerant, inclusive, ethical twenty-first century society.

Chapter 1 makes the case for democratic "stakeholder" participation in educa-tion, drawing on the research into student, teacher and parent voice. Chapters 2, 3 and 4 look at inspiring examples where students, parents and teachers have helped shape their schools and have made a real difference. Chapter 5 brings these three strands together, arguing for each school community to work together to create and realise their own educational vision. This is not a new idea and examples from other countries, where education has a greater connection with the democratic process, are explored in Chapter 6. Finally, Chapter 7 introduces resources, activities and frameworks to support schools in this work.

There is an implicit premise to the book which is that schools need to change in order to meet the needs of young people and of society in our fast-changing and uncertain world. Many educationalists have been saying as much for years. There are countless books documenting the kinds of changes that need to hap-pen. Few, however, talk about the process: *how* to bring about the necessary change. One of the best-known educators of our time – Ken Robinson, author of *Creative Schools* (2015) – argues that:

> we need a revolution in education. Like most revolutions it has been brewing for a long time, and in many places it is already well under way. It is coming, not from the top down; it is coming as it must do, from the ground up.

My hope is that this book makes a small contribution to that revolution.*

Note

*   This book is predominantly about the state sector in England, although it has relevance for many other countries. Scotland, Wales and Northern Ireland have different education systems and whilst they are referred to and case studies from each country are included, the main argument relates to the English system.

For ease of reading, any research or publication referred to in the body of a chapter is included in the references at the end of the chapter.

Bibliography

Ball, S. (2007) *Education plc: Understanding Private Sector Participation in Public Sector Education*. London: Routledge.

Carnie. F. (2017) *Alternative Approaches to Education: A Guide for Teachers and Parents*. London: Routledge.

Dewey, J. (1916) *Democracy and Education*. New York: Macmillan.

Ravitch, D. (2013) *Reign of Error: The Hoax of the Privatization Movement and the Danger to America's Public Schools*. New York: Vintage Books.

Robinson, K. (2015) *Creative Schools*. London: Penguin.

Wilshaw, M. (2016) *Focused Inspections of Academies in Multi-academy Trusts*. London: Ofsted.

Worth, J. (2015) *Analysis of Academy School Performance in GCSEs 2014*. Slough: NFER.

Worth, J. (2016) *Analysis of Academy School Performance in 2015*. Slough: NfER.

1 Key research and contemporary debates

What are the purposes of education and who should decide? These are critical questions for schools, local communities and society, questions which challenge our view of schooling and the role it plays in building the future. They go to the heart of what kind of society we want to create and the role of education in helping to shape it. Do we want a society built on the values of democracy, fairness and respect or one based on competition and the survival of the fittest? These are stark choices but the way schooling is organised influences the values of young people who experience it and, by extension, their priorities for the future.

A fundamental principle of democracy is that individuals should be able to actively participate in decisions that affect their lives. It surely follows that in a healthy democratic society, democratic processes will be incorporated into the education system so that all those who are involved, namely teachers, parents and students, can share in shaping the purposes of education.

As Gert Biesta, Professor of Education at Brunel University, has argued:

> a democratic society is precisely one in which the purpose of education is not given but is a constant topic for discussion and deliberation.

Education inhabits a critical domain since it is about the development of the next generation who will be responsible for shaping society for the future. In order to guarantee the democratic nature of society going forward, it is important therefore to strengthen democratic processes and procedures to make space for the dialogue referred to by Biesta. If governments, which are by nature partisan, dictate the nature and content of schooling it takes away from individuals, schools and communities a significant degree of power and agency over their own lives.

This point is well illustrated by the current situation in England where the school system itself is dominated by the principles of the market and where a narrow vision of education prevails, one which prepares children to contribute to a society and an economy based on neo-liberal, consumerist values. Is it the role of a democratically elected government to prescribe the content of the curriculum and the methods of teaching such that schools turn out young people who will contribute to the perpetuation of the government's political and economic agendas? Alternatively, should education be distanced from the national political arena so that schooling is not organised to serve the ends of any one political party but rather to meet the changing educational and developmental needs of children and young people?

The aim here is not to make a case for an alternative vision of education to that which is promulgated by any particular government but rather to suggest that communities should decide for themselves, democratically, how best to educate their young. In so doing, schools would benefit from the breadth of expertise and imagination that a wide range of stakeholders can bring.

There is an existing international democratic education movement with numerous schools on every continent. It is based on a somewhat different understanding of the person than that which is held by those who subscribe to the traditional transmission-based view of education in that it challenges the centrality of the expert in the learning process. In an article for the American journal, *Education Week* in 2016, Harry Boyte, Head of the Center for Democracy and Citizenship at the University of Minnesota, explained:

> Rather than conceiving of people as needy consumers reducible to market niches and stereotypes, the democracy school philosophy conceives of humans as immensely complex and dynamic, aspiring to co-creative civic agency. Democratic education ... rests on a conviction that humans are creative agents, whose capacities are developed in dynamic relationships.

Put simply, instead of seeing children as an empty vessel to be filled with facts and knowledge, democratic education views them as active participants in their own education.

It will require a major shift to move towards an education system based on democratic principles, but the premise of this book is that in twenty-first-century Britain, this is the direction in which we need to be heading. If we want to strengthen democracy and if we want young people to grow up knowing that their views count, then it is important to start early and ensure that democratic processes are central not just to how schools are governed but to how education takes place on a daily basis within the classroom. In a recent edition of the journal *Forum* (2016), the editor, Howard Stevenson, argued that democracy is "not just about school governance, but [is] central to pedagogical practice".

There is a growing body of research and practice in the fields of student participation, parental involvement and teacher voice which points to the fact that higher levels of school autonomy and greater participation on the part of key stakeholders lead to more positive outcomes for children and young people. This chapter will outline some of that research to show how the involvement of different key groups is central not just to improving our education system but also to creating a more inclusive, equitable and democratic society.

For a moment, let's look at the world outside of education where it is increasingly common for companies, government departments, national agencies and a wide range of service providers to consult their stakeholders. They do this because they have found that it helps them to provide a better service. If they listen to the needs of their customers, clients and partners, they are better able to meet them. They have understood that collaboration helps them to improve their performance. Building good relationships is seen as fundamental to the development of shared values and also to enhancing their reputation.

Responsible organisations have noticed that by paying attention to their stakeholders they can be more responsive and more effective in a world beset by a plethora of challenges: it is not just a case of improving profit margins or minimising costs. The retail chain John Lewis is one of around 100 employee-owned businesses in the UK. A report by the Cass Business School (Lampel et al) comparing such organisations with companies in conventional ownership found that employees that have a stake in the company they work for are more committed to delivering quality and more flexible in the face of the needs of the business.

Consultation and collaboration can contribute to innovation by helping to identify new ways of doing things. It can also assist with the identification and management of risks. And in a world which is increasingly aware of the importance of social equity and sustainable development, such dialogue and engagement is understood to be a central element in demonstrating corporate social responsibility.

This growing trend in stakeholder participation seems to be passing education by at national, local and school level. Where there are attempts at engagement, it is often done in a tokenistic way, or only involves a few of the key players.

Parents have a huge stake in the education system but regardless of this, there is currently no organisation representing them at national level which the government consults as a matter of course when making policy affecting children. At local level, few authorities have a systematic way of consulting parents on local issues. The majority of academy chains also have no mechanism for listening to parents. And at school level, whilst most schools have parent governors on their governing bodies, these governors are under no obligation to consult the parent body as a whole. When they contribute to governing body decision-making, they are representing their own views rather than those of the wider parent body. Some schools have set up parent voice bodies to give parents a say, but numbers are still low and there is no statutory requirement for consultation with parents, even though practically everything that happens in a school affects parents and carers in one way or another.

As far as teachers are concerned, again there is no single professional body representing teachers' views in the development of education policy. The teaching unions all operate at national as well as local levels, but they are often perceived as being concerned mainly with teachers' terms and conditions rather than with fundamental questions about learning and teaching. They often have different priorities and standpoints from each other with the effect that, in England, there is no single representative body which the government can consult in the development of policy. A lack of consultation features at local level, and certainly at school level too. Teachers often say that they do not have a voice in school decision-making. Again, most schools have teacher governors, but as with parents, they do not necessarily consult fellow staff and feedback their views to the governing body. This means that teachers – the educational professionals who are on the front line and have valuable insight into what works well and what is not working in their school – have little opportunity to influence school policy. Many young teachers starting out report frustration about the mechanistic nature of their work, finding that it bears little relation to their reasons for going into education, but have little chance to contribute to discussions about the policy direction of their school. The crisis in teacher retention is a direct corollary of the powerlessness that many teachers feel and the fact that too great a compromise is required in terms of their original motivation for becoming a teacher. It should be asked why we train teachers as professionals and then fail to make use of their expertise.

As for school students, they too do not have a direct representative voice at national or local levels. There is a Children's Commissioner for each of the four nations making up the UK and his or her role is to listen to children on a wide range of issues which affect them and to represent those issues to government. Whilst this is welcome, it is a far cry from the government listening directly to a representative body of children and young people. Some local authorities have developed a young people's forum to give children a voice but these are few and far between. At school level, many institutions have student councils and some have student governors. However, a common complaint from young people is that they are given a say only in low-level matters and do not get the opportunity to contribute to decision-making on bigger issues, in particular, those which affect their learning.

There are of course some exceptions – Brighton and Hove has set up a local Parents and Carers Council so that parents of children with special needs can have a voice in decisions which affect their children. Portsmouth City Council set up the Council of Portsmouth Students ten years ago to facilitate a dialogue between young people and education chiefs on the city council. This has developed into a forum for cross-city debate between young people from all Portsmouth secondary schools. The aim is to be the city-wide voice of young people on education and school improvement matters. And in the Leeds area there are a number of schools in which teachers who are engaged in research projects are consulted in an ongoing way about how to improve outcomes for low-achieving children in their schools. But these are one-offs rather than the norm.

Figure 1.1 Student Voice Day in Portsmouth
Credit: Fiona Carnie

We need to ask why those people who are most involved with education on a day-to-day basis and who are most affected by educational decision-making struggle to contribute to policy discussions at any level. The following sections summarise some of the research which points to the benefits that can accrue to schools from listening to students, teachers and parents.

Student voice

> Parties shall assure to the child who is capable of forming his or her own views the right to express those views freely in all matters affecting the child, the views of the child being given due weight in accordance with the age and maturity of the child.
>
> (United Nations Convention on the Rights of the Child, 1989)

Article 12 of the United Nations Convention on the Rights of the Child, which has been ratified by all countries in the world other than the USA, stipulates that children and young people have the right to have a say on matters which affect them. It also states that children and young people should be given the information they need to enable them to make sound decisions. It should follow on from this that young people are consulted about their education in an age-appropriate way.

The Children and Young People's Commissioner for England has noted the importance of giving school students a voice in decision-making and commissioned a research project to identify the important elements of good practice in this area. The project summary, published in 2011, asserts that "schools see better learning when student voice is included. Giving students control over aspects of their learning leads to much more engagement". The report also recognises the value of student involvement in governors' meetings and suggests having a standing item to hear the student voice on the meeting agenda of school governing bodies or, alternatively, asking a governor to come to school council meetings so that students' views are heard in the process of school decision-making. School ethos is also referred to, drawing attention to the importance of "senior leaders, teachers, teaching assistants, lunchtime staff, students and parents all giving each other a voice and being given respect".

Such strong and clear statements, based on a review of the field, point to the existence of a powerful body of evidence. Indeed, research into student participation which has been carried out over the past two decades indicates the importance of listening to the views of students in the drive to improve schools. A two-year longitudinal study conducted by Professor Jean Rudduck at the University of Cambridge for the Economic and Social Research Council (ESRC) found that when young people are involved in decisions about their learning, they become more motivated and develop a more positive attitude and this in turn helps to improve outcomes. Rudduck's research has been influential in demonstrating that by consulting young people about their learning, teachers gain valuable insight into the teaching and learning process, which helps them to do a better job.

> Evidence from various projects ... suggests that hearing what pupils have to say about teaching, learning and schooling enables teachers to look at things from the pupil's perspective – and the world of school can look very different from this angle ... [It] is the first step towards fundamental change in classrooms and schools.
>
> (Flutter, 2007)

Such work on student participation recognises the importance of changing the role of students from passive recipient to active participant in their education – a significant shift.

These ideas are not new. The research above is predated by the work of the influential philosopher, John Dewey, at the beginning of the twentieth century, who argued that it is not sufficient to teach young people *about* democracy. They have to *do* democracy as an integral part of their daily life in schools and classrooms. Young people need to be involved in decisions about their learning. In addition, through their everyday experiences in the classroom, they can learn to become active citizens and participants in society. At root, this is about the crucial role that education can play in strengthening democracy and society.

Professor Michael Fielding of the Institute of Education has written extensively about student voice, most recently in his book with Peter Moss on *Radical Education and the Common School* (2011). He draws a clear distinction between the kinds of student voice processes in which staff invite and make space for student discussion and decision-making on agreed issues and on terms set by the school, and what he calls "intergenerational learning as lived democracy". Fielding identifies a range of settings, past and present – for example, the staff and pupil panels at St George-in-the East in Stepney in London in the 1940s and 1950s, the Moot at Countesthorpe College in Leicestershire in the 1970s and Hall Meetings at Stantonbury Campus in the 1980s, all schools within the state system – where through such a "lived democracy" students shared, with adults, responsibility for and commitment to the common good. A small number of democratic schools, such as Summerhill and Sands, where adults and students make decisions together about the running of their school, exist today in the UK in the alternative independent sector. Fielding's point, like Dewey's, is that if we are serious about educating children to be democratic citizens then such democratic experiences are an important part of everyday school life for all.

The government has acknowledged the benefits of student voice. In 2014, the Department for Education published guidance for schools on *Listening to and Involving Children and Young People*, which stated that:

> The Government is committed to the promotion and protection of children's rights, in line with the United Nations Convention on the Rights of the Child. It believes that children and young people should have opportunities to express their opinion in matters that affect their lives.

This guidance goes on to recognise that the benefits include encouraging pupils to become active participants in a democratic society as well as contributing to improved achievement and attainment.

Why then is change so slow in coming? In a paper on the *Transformative Power of Student Voice* dating from 2002, Fielding and Rudduck concluded that "we need to respond to the repeated call from students for more responsibility, more opportunities to contribute to decision-making, more opportunities for dialogue about learning and the conditions of learning". But in spite of the research and the pronouncements, the number of schools which genuinely listen to students and involve them in decision-making on issues which matter are few and far between. Those schools which have taken heed of the research, some of which are featured in Chapter 4, have seen significant benefits. But 100 years on from John Dewey's seminal book entitled *Democracy and Education* and in spite of numerous research studies, they remain the exception.

Parent voice

The area of parental engagement is also well researched. Charles Desforges, Emeritus Professor at Exeter University, has written widely about the positive impact that accrues from involving parents in their children's education. The literature review which he carried out with Abouchaar in 2003 found that when parents support their children's learning, this contributes to improved outcomes for the child. Those children who do not have a supportive home environment are at a significant disadvantage. As John Hattie, Professor of Education at the University of Melbourne, found in his 2009 study, the effect of parental engagement over a student's school career is equivalent to adding two to three years to that student's education.

There are a range of ways in which schools can involve parents. The *Review of Best Practice in Parental Engagement* (2010) carried out by Goodall and Vorhaus of the University of Bath on behalf of the Department for Education found that some of the most effective ways in which schools can support parents is to teach them how to support learning at home and also to organise family learning activities in which children and adults can learn together.

Much of the research that has been conducted presupposes that the role of parents is to support the school in educating their child on terms set down by the school. In reality, many parents see their role as somewhat different and whilst wishing to support their child's learning they do not necessarily agree with everything that the school does and may like to be more involved in school decision-making.

A report on *Engaging Parents in Raising Achievement: Do Parents Know They Matter?* by Harris and Goodall at the University of Warwick in 2007 concluded that parental engagement is the most powerful school improvement lever that exists. The authors argued that alongside encouraging parents to support their children's learning, it was also important to involve them in school life. This view was corroborated by a government-funded project (Carnie) on *Setting up a Parent Council*, which found that it can be transformational for schools to involve parents in decision-making. Schools that participated in the project and which consulted parents on a wide range of issues found that such collaboration led to a significant increase in the number of parents who got involved with the school and in the level of their involvement.

There is a particular challenge for schools in terms of reaching disengaged parents. As part of the London Challenge in 2005, Carpentier and Lall of the Institute of Education looked at a number of projects which focused on reaching out to such families. They found that those projects that investigated the barriers which prevented parents from getting involved and then prioritised their needs were more effective. They concluded – somewhat radically – that "schools' needs have to be secondary to the needs of the parents they are trying to engage if they are to be successful". The implication is that the onus is on schools to find out what those needs are.

In a study in 2004 for the Harvard Family Learning Project, Sara Redding and her team of researchers studied parental involvement strategies in 129 schools in areas of high deprivation in the US over a two-year period. They found that "parental involvement in school decision-making contributes to modest but significant achievement gains".

In a chapter for a book on *Reimagining the Purpose of Schools*, published in 2016, Professor Stephen Ball of University College London suggested that:

> tackling the relationship between education, inequality and poverty differently would involve re-connecting education with the lives, hopes and aspirations of children and parents, not through choice and competition but through participation, debate and educative engagement of schools with their communities.

Various studies, including one conducted by Peters, Seeds, Goldstein and Coleman in 2008, have found that over two-thirds of parents would like to get more involved in their child's school life. The research included in this section suggests that if schools are to be able to meet the needs of local families and communities and get the best for their children, it is incumbent on them to listen to parents and work with them in partnership. If parental engagement is a powerful key to school improvement, as indicated, the gains can best be leveraged through collaboration. Some of those schools which are committed to such a partnership approach are discussed in Chapter 4.

Teacher voice

By way of contrast, teacher voice is an area which is relatively under-researched in the UK. Professor Lori Beckett of Leeds Beckett University has researched and written in the journal, *Urban Review*, about a school/university partnership in the north of England where research carried out by teachers has contributed to school improvement policy. Other examples of research focusing on teacher influence on the direction of their school are hard to come by. Beckett refers to such "practical-pedagogical work done against the odds to advocate more realistic policies and practices" as a struggle. Surely it should be the norm. She is clear about the benefits in terms of building an evidence base, contributing to research-informed teaching and the co-construction of school action plans that are in line with a school's context.

There are more examples of research into teacher voice in America and different studies indicate that it is of central importance in the creation of a positive school climate. Richard Kahlenberg, a Senior Fellow at the Century Foundation, an American think tank, argues that when teachers are encouraged to collaborate with each other and are able to participate in school decision-making, this leads to a better learning environment for students which, in turn, helps to raise attainment. In an article written with H. Potter for the American Federation of Teachers in 2014, he claimed that teacher voice has been found to contribute to creating a better working environment for teachers, which is key to keeping teachers in the profession.

In an article, *Short on Power, Long on Responsibility*, published in the journal, *Education Leadership* in 2007, Richard Ingersoll, an American researcher on teacher workplace issues, saw teachers as caught in the middle between the competing demands of school leaders and students. This raises questions as to why there should be such a conflict but supports the argument for sufficient autonomy for teachers to be able to mediate between the two. Ingersoll found that:

> schools in which teachers have more control over key school-wide and classroom decisions have fewer problems with student misbehaviour, show more collegiality and cooperation among teachers and administrators [school leaders], have a more committed and engaged teaching staff, and do a better job of retaining their teachers.

Teacher collaboration does indeed seem to be of central importance. In his book *Beyond the Education Wars* (2013), Greg Anrig suggests that "one of the most important ingredients in successful schools is the inverse of conflict: intensive collaboration amongst administrators [school leaders] and teachers, built on a shared sense of mission and focused on improved student learning".

A longitudinal study carried out in American secondary schools, as reported by Lee and Smith in 1996 in an article for the *American Journal of Education*, found that students do better in all subjects when teachers collaborate and take collective responsibility for student learning. In Finland too, a country which has consistently scored well in the OECD PISA rankings, the teaching profession is highly regarded and the culture in schools is one of collaboration and shared responsibility. The American research and studies from Finland both point to more equitable outcomes for students when teachers have a voice in school decision-making. The study by Lee and Smith indicates that where there is increased staff responsibility and collegiality, the gap in achievement between children from different socio-economic backgrounds is reduced. A second longitudinal study conducted by the University of Chicago Consortium on School Research over a period of 15 years in hundreds of elementary [primary] schools in Chicago found that those schools which improved the most were those with a focus on staff collegiality and professional development.

In the drive to ensure that schools can best meet the needs of their students and families, it makes sense to listen to those on the front line and take account of their views in school decision-making. The Finnish educator, Pasi Sahlberg, has talked about the need to build a culture of responsibility and trust within the education system where teacher professionalism is valued in judging what is best for students. It can be argued that school leaders in England have so little room for manoeuvre due to the unremitting focus on test scores of both the government and Ofsted, that they are inhibited from truly listening to their staff on matters concerning the overarching vision and direction of the school. Some examples of schools which do give weight to the views of teachers are included as case studies in Chapter 2.

Challenges

It is clear that there are significant challenges for schools wishing to listen to the many and varied voices within their communities. Firstly, there is a lack of training for teachers in the areas of both student participation and parental engagement. School leadership training also pays scant attention to the notion of voice. Whilst the concept of distributed leadership, whereby leadership is shared rather than concentrated at the top, has been promoted for well over a decade, if professionals do not understand how to listen and respond to different voices within the school community in ways that will help to move the school forward positively, then it is likely that they will minimise opportunities for those voices to be heard.

Secondly, the school culture in England is not one which foregrounds participation. School students expect to be told what and how to learn. As far as parents are concerned, there is still widespread understanding that you leave your child at the school gates and it is the school's job to educate him or her. As for teachers, whilst many young people enrol on teacher training courses with a strong motivation to help improve the lives of young people, once in their first jobs they soon realise that their sphere of influence is restricted to the classroom and their dealings with their students and that they have little say on the school's values, vision and direction.

This leads to a third area of difficulty which concerns the question of competing agendas. Many teachers question the extent to which they can encourage students to make their voices heard since they themselves have no voice. Ideas and wishes expressed by students may be entirely reasonable but completely unrealisable within the framework of the school. As American researcher, Cook-Sather, has cautioned in her 2002 article on *Authorizing Students' Perspectives*, listening to students' voices must not come at the expense of teachers' voices. Demands from parents similarly might be comprehensible but may also put too great a strain on teachers who are already overstretched, and vice versa. How likely is it that students, parents and teachers will have the same priorities – and how can parents and schools be sure that the expectations they have of each other are reasonable? There is an implicit challenge for schools in terms of how they mediate the differing views that are expressed.

There is a fourth and very significant challenge in terms of creating environments in which people are encouraged to express their views and that is the issue of size: size of classes and size of schools. Many teachers would argue that they have too many students in their class to be able to allocate sufficient time to listen to each one. For students too, large classes can be intimidating and many choose to keep quiet rather than expose themselves by talking about issues which matter to them. The experience of parents' evenings illustrates well the challenges for teachers in engaging in meaningful dialogue with the parents of each of their students. Large schools make it difficult to build a listening culture in which all people – staff, students and parents – feel heard and valued. Our factory model of schooling is not conducive to building a collaborative ethos. Research on school size and class size – much of it American – which has been summarised separately by Wasley (2002) and Tasker (2003, 2008) – indicates the importance of smaller educational structures in the creation of a more democratic system.

Such challenges, whilst real and understandable, do not provide sufficient reason to sideline democratic approaches. As Winston Churchill observed, democracy is a far from perfect system of government: it is just that it is the least bad option. And the business of schools is messy. There are different ways in which learning can be organised and no right answers. The bottom line though is that what we have at the moment is not working for too many people, most of all for many children and young people, but also, arguably for society.

But there are ways forward. A more participative approach to school decision-making can address the isolation that many within the education system feel. The following three chapters explore examples of voice and participation from the perspectives of teachers, students and parents with a view to showing how an organisational framework which prioritises dialogue and shared decision-making can produce remarkable outcomes for all.

Bibliography

Anrig, G. (2013) *Beyond the Education Wars: Evidence That Collaboration Builds Effective Schools*. New York: Century Foundation Press.

Apple, M. and Beane, J. (2007) *Democratic Schools: Lessons in Powerful Education*, 2nd edition. Portsmouth, NH: Heinemann.

Ball, S. (2016) Education, Justice and Democracy: The Struggle over Ignorance and Opportunity in A. Montgomery and I. Kehoe (eds.), *Reimagining the Purpose of Schools*. Switzerland: Springer.

Beckett, L. (2014) Raising Teachers' Voice on Achievement in Urban Schools in England: An Introduction. *Urban Review*, 46(5): 783-799.

Biesta, G. (2007) Why "What Works" Won't Work: Evidence-based Practice and the Democratic Deficit in Educational Research. *Educational Theory*, 57(1): 1-22.

Boyte, H. (2016) Democracy Schools After the Election: Overcoming the Cult of the Expert. *Education Week*, issue 11, November 2016.

Brighouse, T. (2017) Britain's four school systems all march to a different drumbeat. *The Guardian*, 27 February 2017.

Bryk, A.S., Sebring, P.B., Allensworth, E., Luppescu, S. and Easton, J.Q. (2010) *Organizing Schools for Improvement: Lessons from Chicago*. Chicago: University of Chicago Press.

Carnie, F. (2006) *Setting up a Parent Council: Case Studies*. London: DfES.

Carpentier, V. and Lall, M. (2005) *Review of Successful Parental Involvement Practices for 'Hard to Reach' Parents.* London: Institute of Education.

Cook-Sather, A. (2002) Authorizing Students' Perspectives: Towards Trust, Dialogue, and Change in Education. *Educational Researcher,* 31(4): 3-14.

Department for Education (DfE) (2014) *Listening to and Involving Children and Young People Guidance.* Available at: www.gov.uk/government/uploads/system/uploads/attachment_data/file/437241/Listening_to_and_involving_children_and_young_people.pdf

Department for Education (DfE) (2016) *Educational Excellence Everywhere.* White paper. London: HMSO.

Desforges, C. and Abouchaar, A. (2003) *The Impact of Parental Involvement, Parental Support and Family Education on Pupil Achievement and Adjustment: A Literature Review.* London: Queen's Printer.

Dewey, J. (1916) *Democracy and Education.* New York: Macmillan.

Fielding, M. and Moss, P. (2011) *Radical Education and the Common School: A Democratic Alternative.* London: Routledge.

Fielding, M. and Rudduck, J. (2002) *The Transformative Power of Student Voice: Confronting the Power Issues.* Paper presented at the Annual Conference of the British Educational Research Association, University of Exeter, England, 12-14 September 2002.

Flutter, J. (2007) Developing Pupil Voice Strategies to Improve Classroom Practice. *Learning and Teaching Update,* 3: 5-7.

Goodall, J. and Vorhaus, J. (2010) *Review of Best Practice in Parental Engagement.* London: DfE.

Harris, A. and Goodall, J. (2007) *Engaging Parents in Raising Achievement: Do Parents Know They Matter?* London: DCSF.

Hattie, J. (2009) *Visible Learning: A Synthesis of over 800 Meta-Analyses Relating to Achievement.* London: Routledge.

Ingersoll, R.M. (2007) Short on Power, Long on Responsibility. *Educational Leadership,* 65(1): 20-25.

Kahlenberg, R.D. and Potter, H (2014) Why Teacher Voice Matters. *American Educator,* Winter 2014-2015.

Lampel, J., Bhalla, A. and Chordia, M. (2014) *Does Employee Ownership Confer Long-term Resilience?* London: Cass Business School.

Lee, V. and Smith, J. (1996) Collective Responsibility for Learning and Its Effects on Gains in Achievement for Early Secondary School Students. *American Journal of Education,* 104(2): 103-147.

Manzone, J. (2016) Factory-farmed Teachers Will Fail Our Children. *Forum,* 58(2): 253-256.

Peters, M., Seeds, K., Goldstein, A. and Coleman, N. (2008) *Parental Involvement in Children's Education Research Report RR034.* London: DCSF.

Redding, S., Langdon, J., Meyer, J. and Sheley, P. (2004) *The Effects of Comprehensive Parent Engagement on Student Learning Outcomes.* Paper presented to American Educational Research Association, Massachussetts: Harvard Family Learning Project.

Rudduck, J. and Flutter, J. (2003) *How to Improve your School: Giving Pupils a Voice,* London and New York: Continuum.

Rudduck, J. and McIntyre, D. (2007) *Improving Learning Through Consulting Pupils.* London: Routledge.

Sahlberg, P. (2010) *Global Education Reform Movement and National Educational Change.* Presentation to EUNEC Conference, Brussels.

Sahlberg, P. (2015) *Finnish Lessons.* New York: Teachers College Press.

Stevenson, H. (2016) The Time Is Now: Reconstructing High Quality, Democratic, Public Education. *Forum,* 58(2): 129-134.

Tasker, M. (2003) *Smaller Stuctures in Secondary Education: A Research Digest.* Bristol: Human Scale Education.

Tasker, M. (2008) *Human Scale Education: History, Values and Practice.* Bristol: Human Scale Education.

Wasley, P. (2002) School Size. Small Classes, Small School: The Time is Now. Educational Leadership, 59(5):6-10.

Websites

Alternatives in Education www.alternativesineducation.org
Children's Commissioner for England www.childrenscommissioner.gov.uk/
   Report on *Student Voice for Schools – How to Guide* commissioned by the Office of the Children's Commissioner for England http://involver.org.uk/wp-content/uploads/down-loads/2011/09/Involver_-_How_to_Guide_Student_voice_for_schools.pdf
Collective Leadership Institute www.collectiveleadership.de/apex/cli/home/
EUNEC www.eunec.eu/
   Report on *Participant and Stakeholder Involvement in Education Policy Making* www.eunec.eu/sites/www.eunec.eu/files/event/attachments/report_brussels.pdf
International Democratic Education Network www.idenetwork.org/
United Nations Convention on the Rights of the Child www.ohchr.org/EN/ProfessionalInterest/Pages/CRC.aspx

2 Teacher voice
Listening to the professionals

There is a growing crisis in the teaching profession in England. A recent report from the House of Commons Education Committee acknowledged the shortage of teachers in a number of subjects and geographical areas, the difficulty in recruiting new teachers and the problems caused by the continuing exodus both of older teachers taking early retirement and younger teachers. Around 30 per cent of new teachers leave the profession within five years of qualifying. The government is consistently failing to meet its recruitment and retention targets and this is putting increasing pressure on schools.

The report, published in 2017, recognised some of the reasons for the problems:

> Over the past six years schools have been faced with a series of changes to curriculum, assessment and the accountability system, as well as uncertainty about changes to school structures. This will have led to increased workload and pressure as schools implement the changes.

Responding to a survey called *Why Teach?* which was carried out by Menzies in 2015, 76 per cent of teachers cited high workload as the most common reason for considering leaving the profession. Teachers spend increasing amounts of time ticking boxes, entering data and performing other routine tasks to ensure that their school can meet its legal accountability responsibilities. In her submission to the House of Commons Committee, Alison Peacock, Chief Executive of the recently established Chartered College of Teaching, claimed that "workload is inextricably linked to the accountability agenda".

This view is endorsed by numerous academics, school leaders and teachers across the country who have, for years, been claiming that the testing and accountability framework has put schools in a stranglehold, exerting too much pressure on staff and students alike. There are few signs, however, that the government is listening to these voices. As recently as 2016, the *Times Educational Supplement* reported, in an article by Helen Ward, that changes to primary assessment were "chaotic" and causing upheaval within the sector and that these changes had not been endorsed by the profession.

The overarching problem is that education is so tightly managed and controlled by central government that schools have limited freedom to act in what they believe to be the best interests of their students. The mantra from policymakers is that the academisation agenda has freed schools and given them greater autonomy. But with all maintained schools being subject to the strict inspection regime conducted by Ofsted, there is little room for manoeuvre. Not only does it create a heavy administrative burden for teachers, it also leaves school leaders and teachers powerless to introduce new approaches unless they are guaranteed to deliver the outcomes that Ofsted is looking for, namely the narrow academic achievements prioritised by the government. In spite of the best efforts of the vast majority of school staff, this overbearing control has reduced learning and teaching to a joyless act of information delivery, undermining the role of the teacher in the process.

The limitations of such a test-based system are well-expressed in *Manifesto 15*, a charter drawn up in America in 2015 by educationalist John Moravec and endorsed by educationalists around the world:

> **We cannot manage knowledge.** When we talk about knowledge and innovation, we frequently commingle or confuse the concepts with data and information instead. Too often, we fool ourselves into thinking that we give kids knowledge, when we are just testing them for what information they can repeat. To be clear: data are bits and pieces here and there, which we combine into information. Knowledge is about taking information and creating meaning at a personal level. We innovate when we take action with what we know to create new value. Understanding this difference exposes one of the greatest problems facing school management and teaching: while we are good at managing information, we simply cannot manage the knowledge in students' heads without degrading it back to information.

The problems are not unconnected with the increasingly fractured teacher training framework in England. There are many routes into teaching nowadays, but most are too short to equip new teachers with the knowledge, skills and understanding of child development that are required for such a complex job. By contrast, teacher education in a number of other European countries such as Finland, Denmark, Germany and the Netherlands – all of which outperformed England in the 2015 PISA tests – is much lengthier and more comprehensive. In these countries, teacher education courses are generally four or five years long and cover important areas such as child development, educational theory and different pedagogical approaches as well as giving students extensive practical experience with opportunities to reflect on what they have learned during their placements. Contrast this with the hurried ten months that many trainee teachers experience in England.

The House of Commons Education Committee referred to above was also advised that practising teachers in England receive very little professional development compared to those in other European countries. All schools offer staff training but too often it is of poor quality and is not personalised to meet individual teachers' needs. The end result is that our teachers feel less well prepared than their counterparts elsewhere, which in turn leads them to struggle more with their work.

In his report for the OECD on *Building a High-Quality Teaching Profession: Lessons from around the World* (2011), Education Director, Andreas Schleicher, draws attention to the importance of high-quality teacher recruitment and initial teacher education in order to build a profession that is able to respond to changing demands. He also points to the need for well-tailored professional development programmes for practising teachers as well as opportunities for collaborative learning so that teachers can share good practice and learn from each other. This report posits that teachers must be properly prepared so that they can play a central and positive role in bringing about educational change. As London primary school teacher Jane Manzone comments in her 2016 article in *Schools Week* on 'Factory-farmed Teachers':

> We need to grow our teachers slowly and support them as they develop. A young teacher must still answer the very important questions: What is education for? What kind of teacher am I? Such questions are of vital importance.

It would appear though that the government does not trust teachers with the education of the next generation. Why else would an entire workforce be deprofessionalised in the way that has progressively occurred over the past three decades, since the introduction of the national curriculum and the SATS? Howard Stevenson, Professor of Educational Leadership at Nottingham University, makes the connection with the neo-liberal, privatisation agenda and in a chapter written with Alison Gilliland of the Irish National Teachers' organisation entitled *The Teachers' Voice: Teacher Unions at the Heart of a new Democratic Professionalism* (2016) argues that:

> A key feature of the market-driven GERM [Global Education Reform Movement] is its intent to break-up and fragment, as a deliberate attempt to undermine the influence of professional interests within public education systems.

The systematic dumbing down of the profession in England has had other consequences and may have contributed to a reduction in respect for teachers. In its submission to the House of Commons Education Committee on The Recruitment and Retention of Teachers, academics from the Institute of Education wrote:

> ultimately, the status accorded to teaching is an important factor in attracting and retaining high calibre candidates. According to the OECD, 35% of

Figure 2.1 Teachers' meeting at a Finnish school
Credit: Kilpinen School, Finland

teachers in England feel their profession is valued by society, compared with 66% in Korea and 60% in Finland.

If there is to be any hope of transforming the life chances of children and of reducing social inequalities, we need a teaching workforce that is confident, well-trained and trusted rather than demoralised, overburdened and under-prepared. Whilst Schleicher argues for a collaborative model of reform in which teachers play a key part, successive Secretaries of State at the Department of Education have chosen the opposite path: a top-down model that is conceived and imposed from the centre.

In Wales, where education is currently undergoing an in-depth review to rewrite the curriculum and review assessment procedures, the Welsh government has recently commissioned a review of its progress from the OECD. In its report, published in 2017, researchers commented that "in the future Wales will need a different type of teaching professional; one who has significantly more responsibility and understands the 'why' and the 'how' as well as the 'what'".

In Scotland, the Curriculum for Excellence (Scotland's skills-based curriculum), introduced in 2010, moved away from a top-down model of change to an approach which sees teachers as playing a central role. They are encouraged to be reflective practitioners who can share and develop ideas within their schools. A new National Improvement Framework introduced in 2016 cited teacher professionalism as one of the key drivers of improvement.

The question for all who are concerned with education – and one that is frequently articulated is: How can the tide be turned so that teachers feel valued and gain the support that they need to be the best that they can? This is where teacher voice comes in.

A good start might be to create opportunities for discussion and collaboration within schools to mitigate the professional isolation that many staff feel. Not just opportunities to talk about their work, but opportunities to discuss the values, vision and direction of their school in order to develop a shared sense of purpose. Time needs to be set aside for this as happens, for example, in Finland.

Many teachers went into teaching with high ideals. This motivation can be kept alive by encouraging ongoing reflection about school policies and the ways in which these facilitate the positive development of the school. For too long the majority of teachers have been excluded from such debate as it has been the preserve of school leaders and governors. Surely as some of the key stakeholders in a school they need to have a greater sense of ownership over their working environment and practices. Whilst most schools have teacher representation on their governing bodies, their position is rarely one that is given much weight.

As reported in Chapter 1, American studies find that when teachers are involved in school decisions and collaborate with school leaders and with each other, the school climate improves. This promotes a better learning environment for students, which raises student achievement, and a better working environment for teachers, which reduces teacher turnover. This indicates that schools have everything to gain from developing a more reflective and a more participative ethos. According to researcher Richard Ingersoll, data from the Schools and Staffing Survey administered by the US Department of Education's National Center for Education Statistics shows that as teacher control over "social decisions" (such as student discipline and teacher professional development policies) increases, the amount of conflict between students and staff, amongst teachers, and between teachers and the principal all decrease.

This resonates with research from Biesta, Priestley and Robinson at the University of Stirling carried out as part of an ESRC project on *Teacher Agency and Curriculum Change* (2011–12). Biesta points to the importance of relationships in the building of a collaborative culture which enables teachers to take responsibility and develop a sense of agency in their work. Studies he conducted in schools in Scotland which have introduced the Curriculum for Excellence indicate the value of less hierarchical school management structures to enable teachers "to address the complexities encountered in their implementation of a new curriculum". In Scotland, education policy supports teachers to become agents of change and so it is valuable to look at the factors that make this possible.

Some of the messages that can be taken from the reports and studies mentioned above are that teachers need to be valued, adequately trained, given time to do their work properly and time to collaborate with others. Listening to what teachers have to say, interrogating them about their professional lives, their day-to-day experience in the classroom and the support they need to address the challenges they face on a daily basis would be a good starting point to address the crisis in the profession. It is not a tokenistic, phoney form of consultation that is required but a genuine dialogue at all levels. At national level, policymakers have everything to gain from hearing from those on the ground and reflecting what they hear in education decision-making. Teachers are at the heart of our school system and are thus key stakeholders to be consulted in the development of policies which they play such an integral part in delivering.

At the moment, the mechanisms by which the government listens to teachers are inadequate. In theory, the unions could represent the profession in this way, but currently they do not provide a vehicle for teachers' voices to be meaningfully heard. In the eyes of many, they have become discredited by focusing too narrowly on pay and conditions and their methods have often seemed confrontational. There are too many of them and historically, it is arguable that they have not worked hard enough to provide a united and coherent response to education policy.

In the chapter from the book *Flip the System: Changing Education from the Ground Up* cited above, Stevenson and Gilliland see the teaching profession as uniquely positioned to influence and "flip" the education system. This can only be achieved, they argue:

> if teachers organise collectively. Teacher unions therefore, as the independent and democratic organisations that represent teachers' collective voice, are not only at the heart of a new democratic professionalism, but must be central to both making the case for it and mobilising teachers to achieve it.

The democratic professionalism that they talk about refers to activity in three areas, namely:

- shaping conditions for learning and teaching
- developing and enacting policy
- enhancing pedagogical knowledge and professional learning

At the time of writing, there are plans for the two largest teacher unions, NUT and ATL, to merge, as reported in the *Times Educational Supplement* on 22 March 2017, so that they can speak with one voice in "standing up for education, teachers, the wider education profession and for the children and young people we teach". Working together there is an opportunity for them to perform the enhanced role envisaged by Stevenson and Gilliland.

With the establishment of the Chartered College of Teaching in 2016, there is a further opportunity for teachers to be heard at national level. The College, which sees itself as "the collective voice for the profession" is likely to have the ear of government since it is being funded by the Department for Education. However, in gathering teachers' views and representing the profession in policy discussions it will be vital, in the interests of democracy, that it demonstrates its independence.

The key point then is that at national level, government needs to listen seriously to teachers.

But it is time too for a cultural shift at school level so that teachers have a voice in school decision-making. Many teachers are encouraged to undertake action research on a specific issue and present their findings to their colleagues. These findings may affect decisions relating to their particular area of focus. But rarely do teachers feel as though they are genuine partners in the development of school policy as a whole. In carrying out the research for this book, it was extremely hard to find any who felt that they were consulted about their school's vision, its overall direction of travel and related policy decisions.

What changes could be made to ensure that teachers are treated as valued partners?

An enhanced role for teacher governors

Firstly, teachers can be given a more meaningful role on school governing bodies. Decisions made by senior leaders and governors need to take account of the everyday realities of teachers' experiences in the classroom in order for policies to be both workable and supported by all staff. An increase in the number of teacher governors and a rise in their status would enable them to represent the views of their colleagues in discussions.

With such an enhanced role, teacher governors would have the responsibility of gathering, synthesising and reporting on the views of their colleagues at governing body meetings. Either staff meetings could be used to agree on the key messages to feedback or, as an alternative, larger schools might consider setting up a staff council or similar body to ensure that all teachers and support staff have the opportunity to contribute their views. Such staff councils are rare in British schools; they are more common in higher education – there is one at St Andrews University in Scotland for instance – and in some schools overseas.

Staff councils

The purpose of a staff council is to discuss general issues and recommend changes or improvements to school policies. In theory, staff meetings should do this, but more often they become bogged down in the minutiae of operational issues so that discussions bear little relation to the overarching mission and direction of the school. Issues that are under discussion by the governing body and school leadership could be brought to staff council meetings to ensure that staff views feed into the decision-making process. Similarly, issues and concerns raised by staff could be reported to the governing body. It is telling that when most schools now have student councils and a growing number are setting up parent councils or forums, staff do not as a matter of course have the opportunity to influence school policy in an ongoing way. In recognition of the need to build a more collaborative and more democratic school culture, this has to be addressed.

School self-evaluation

A third option is to involve all teachers in a school in a meaningful school self-evaluation process to review what the school is seeking to achieve for its students and assess the degree to which its practices enable it to succeed. In Scotland, the *How Good is Our School?* self-evaluation tool is designed to involve all staff (as well as students and parents) in reflection on the school's strengths and areas for improvement. By sharing responsibility for school improvement in this way, teachers develop a sense of ownership over their working environment.

There are thus a range of things that schools can do to enable school staff to have some autonomy and give them a voice, alongside school leaders, governors, parents and students. By building a strong school community in which teachers play a leading part by contributing their knowledge and expertise, schools will be in a better position to challenge the hegemony of central government. The following case studies give examples of schools where teachers are valued as partners in the school development process.

CASE STUDIES

Case Study 1

Teachers at Stanley Park High School are involved in developing an innovative curriculum and assessment procedures. They are also able to trial different pedagogical approaches in order to best meet the needs of their students.

> **Teacher voice at Stanley Park High School, London Borough of Sutton**
>
> Stanley Park High School – TES Secondary School of the Year 2016 – is a non-selective secondary school in the highly selective borough of Sutton. The school has over 1,100 students across Key Stages 3 to 5 and in 2006 was designated a Building Schools for the Future 'One School Pathfinder' and was charged with being innovative across all aspects of schooling. In

2012, Stanley Park High moved to a new building with an aim to provide a twenty-first-century education which centres on the importance of relationships.

A key structure in fostering excellent relationships is the 'schools-within-schools' model. When pupils arrive at Stanley Park in Year 7 they are placed into one of four mini schools and will remain in those schools throughout their school life. Pupils are divided equally into Trade, Performance and World, with a separate school, Horizon, for students with Autistic Spectrum Condition (ASC). Each mini school is located in a separate part of the building.

Trust is critical at Stanley Park. Both students and teachers are trusted. Teachers are encouraged to take risks alongside the students and this positive relationship-building benefits everyone.

The curriculum approach is governed by the motto 'Igniting a Passion for Learning'. At the heart of this is our bespoke curriculum for Year 7 and 8: the Excellent Futures Curriculum (EFC). In each mini school, English, maths, science, PE, languages and music are taught separately and everything else is taught in our mixed-ability project-based EFC lessons, a programme designed by the school's teachers and leadership team.

We are fortunate as teachers that we are given the freedom to design aspects of the project-based learning curriculum and explore different pedagogical approaches. We can do this with the support of our senior leaders who actively encourage us to push boundaries and try new things.

When I started at Stanley Park High I was given the opportunity to teach the EFC. As a teacher there is nothing more rewarding then seeing students embark on a voyage of discovery and knowing you have been instrumental in facilitating that journey. Walking into an EFC studio you will see students engaged in real-world projects and developing their passion for learning. Teachers take risks, facilitate learning and encourage independent thinking. Every day is different.

As a teacher of the EFC I was given the opportunity to lead and develop the curriculum. This meant having the chance to work with other members of the team to shape the projects we were teaching. Not only were we able to determine the project content and outcomes, we have also been given the freedom to develop the assessment process to ensure it is suitable for our students. We are able to teach to our passions and ensure that the students are motivated and engaged with their learning. A key element of this development has been the chance for us to visit other schools, work with other teachers and take part in a range of training opportunities. Along with three other EFC teachers, I took part in in-depth project-based learning training, which we then went on to implement at the school.

Having the opportunity to visit other schools and open our minds to new pedagogical approaches is key to teacher voice. As a new member of staff I was encouraged to delve beyond a set of pre-determined expectations and challenge what I thought was meant by good teaching. I have subsequently been able to discuss these ideas and implement them in the school environment. After teaching at Stanley Park for only two years, I participated in a study tour to Reykjavik, Iceland in order to visit a range of schools.

These visits had been operating at Stanley Park for at least six years before I joined and teachers have been encouraged to visit schools, both in the UK and abroad, to help create and develop innovative practice. Teachers go on such visits, sometimes with students, to discuss with open minds what is impressive about other schools and what good practice we can adopt for our own community. During the visit to Iceland I had many discussions with the head teacher and another senior member of staff about what we had seen. Having had time to reflect and discuss, we decided we wanted to develop more independence in student learning and I was given the opportunity to launch a brand new Year 7 independent project.

Two years later, I visited a school in San Diego to look closely at their project-based learning model. Again during the study tour I was heavily involved in discussions about improving our own practice both at a classroom level and also at a whole school level. One of the practices we observed there led us to develop our Student Led Conferences, which now have a regular place in the assessment process instead of parents' evenings. These highly praised and widely acclaimed celebrations of a child's achievements allow the pupils to take ownership and articulate their learning. The introduction of Student Led Conferences is a good example of how our school allows teachers to take an idea and develop it in line with the ethos and the vision of the school.

Additionally, Stanley Park High, through its Innovation and Research Academy, SPIRA, regularly welcomes teachers from across the UK and from overseas. This is very useful to us as practitioners in terms of learning from others and sharing our successes.

Our motto 'Igniting a Passion for Learning' applies not just to the students, but to teachers and the whole school community.

Katie Alden, Teacher

www.stanleyparkhigh.org.uk/

Figure 2.2 Students working on the Excellent Futures Curriculum at Stanley Park High
Credit: Russell Sach

Case Study 2

Morpeth School shows that placing trust in the professionalism of teachers and supporting them in their professional development journey pays dividends in terms of improving outcomes for students.

Trusting the professionals at Morpeth School, Bethnal Green, London

Going back to the turn of the century, Morpeth, as with many schools, faced a situation in which levels of attainment were at an unacceptably low level. The school is situated in Bethnal Green, East London and the pupils come from working-class backgrounds with high levels of deprivation. Much change was required and from the outset decisions had to be made regarding the balance between top-down management and the role of the staff in the running of the school. It would be easy with hindsight to pretend that this was clearly thought through but the reality was that our strategy evolved over time. It was, however, based on a strong underlying belief in the importance of engaging and involving the staff. This was much less to do with decisions being taken 'democratically' in the staffroom than a belief in the professionalism of our teachers.

The school went through several stages in its development and although not strictly sequential it is helpful to think of the journey in this way. Initially, systems, structures and behaviour for learning needed to be secure, and in this there was a necessity for strong direction from the school's leadership team. Had this not been present, teacher input and energy would have lacked the support necessary to produce the improvement required. The next stage involved a change in school culture focused on raising expectations and aspirations. This happened in our everyday practice but also through a wide range of enrichment opportunities beyond the classroom which created the educational capital that working-class children frequently lack. Without 'buy-in' from staff this would have been impossible. Improvements in attainment followed but it became increasingly clear that further progress could only come, in this, our most recent stage, from a focus on teaching and learning, from the growth of our teachers and their professional development.

As a school system matures and moves from good to excellent, more and more responsibility is generally passed from the centre to the schools, from the leaders and managers to the teachers. This runs counter to the practice found in some English schools at present where the emphasis is still firmly on directive management, on monitoring teacher performance, on target-setting and on very high levels of accountability. Our view at Morpeth was that whilst this latter approach might be necessary in a struggling school in need of the structure that is mentioned above, it was not going to lead to genuinely outstanding teaching and learning, and equally importantly it was unlikely to result in high staff morale.

Our belief was that our teachers had joined the profession to 'make a difference' and wanted to continually improve their practice. In a staff survey, quality professional development came out as valued more highly than salary or other conditions of service. We developed a system based on trust and a major role is now played by the Teaching and Learning Working Group where, for example, much of the work on developing the school's new Key Stage 3 assessment model was devised and where key priorities such as oracy are developed by the staff. Similarly, a clearer whole school marking policy was requested by middle leaders and this was modelled on the best practice already in place in some departments. As a result of this approach, attainment outcomes have continued to rise and we have been graded Outstanding by Ofsted at two inspections.

However, one of our other leadership principles is that we should always be looking for the next improvement, particularly at the point when the school is doing well. The balance between trust and accountability needs continuous attention. We had always realised that the 'trust model' required intervention with the very small number of staff who didn't respond positively, but we also needed to recognise that even for the majority of staff we had a crucial role in setting the key parameters and ensuring that external changes in policy were being reflected in practice.

Positioning a school on this continuum from total management control to total trust in the professionalism of teachers is a key challenge for leadership. How do you find the balance? Our experience would suggest that the starting point, if we want outstanding schools in which our pupils not only achieve highly but also develop as independent learners, should be based on a belief in our teachers as professionals committed to improving their practice. It is very hard to build an institution with two cultures, one for the pupils where we want creativity, independent thinking and a willingness to challenge, and another for the staff where we tell them what to do. In the same way that the teacher should create a secure environment in which learning can take place, so should the leadership do the same for the whole school, showing trust in the professionalism of their staff but also providing direction, support and challenge.

Jemima Reilly, Head teacher (2013 - present) and Alasdair Macdonald, Head teacher (1992-2013)

http://morpethschool.org.uk/

Case Study 3

As the Oxford Montessori Schools are outside the maintained system, teachers have the freedom to develop their own curricula and lessons. Such teacher autonomy enables staff to personalise learning in order to meet the needs of their students.

Freedom to teach at Oxford Montessori School

Oxford Montessori School (OMS) is an extremely small school for children aged two to 16 years, situated atop a rural hill just outside Oxford. It prides itself on offering a different kind of education, where learning is more relaxed and informal and in which children are able to have freer, more individualised learning experiences. Whilst not as fully democratic or liberalised as schools like Summerhill or Sudbury schools, OMS shares a number of features with these kinds of alternative models of schooling. Alternative education often comes at a cost – literally – in that in order to acquire enough of the desired freedoms, a school generally has to step outside the state system and become fee-paying. Although relatively inexpensive, the OMS model is thus largely unavailable to the most deprived in society, but the school sees itself as something of a laboratory for educational innovation and the hope is that what works for OMS may be useful for others. Over many years, the school has demonstrated a key principle: more trust allows teachers to focus on individual needs and to promote positive mental health, thereby reducing educational inequalities.

As with most alternative education providers, OMS emphasises the importance of trusting that children can be autonomous and self-directed, but it is also vital that the same freedoms are afforded to our teachers. Teachers at the school have been given complete freedom to develop curricula and lessons in a style that they feel is best, and have very minimal pedagogical requirements imposed on them. Since the school has a single teacher per subject, each has almost complete responsibility for teaching and learning in their subject area and is granted the associated rights and responsibilities. Teachers are made aware that they are the experts in the teaching of their subject and that decisions about pedagogy, curriculum content and assessment are – assuming they do not wildly deviate from the school ethos – entirely their own to make. With a significant proportion of the school's intake having special educational needs and mental health conditions, this means that teachers can take rapid and targeted action to support students using approaches that align with their strengths and preferences.

Even OMS is not immune from the need to have some standardisation, particularly in matters that impact on inspection outcomes. Crucially, however, teachers are very much involved in a process of genuine consultation in these cases. Where the school's management have decided on standardised data recording processes, such as for submitting termly plans, teachers have been given opportunities to redraft documents to make them better suited to their needs. Furthermore, the school is increasingly inclined to delegate such tasks to classroom teachers themselves, who are felt to be in a better position to identify what approaches will most benefit students and teachers. This approach has the added benefit of meaning that teachers can benefit from shared resources which they have ownership of and thus feel to be worth using.

By removing micromanagement from above, teachers are more able to relax and enjoy their work. Teachers report a sense that their work is less pressured and that they have more mental space to reflect. In an environment where experimentation is encouraged and enabled, teachers can develop professionally by trying out innovative approaches, safe in the knowledge that they will be trusted to do so and that the learning value even of making mistakes is fully understood. This sense of autonomy and professional growth has been linked to increased job satisfaction (Bogler, 2001) and means that the school is better able to retain effective and motivated teachers.

Happier, less stressed teachers make for a more positive school environment for students and mean that the school has become popular with parents who had found that mainstream education was anxiety-inducing and mentally exhausting for their children. OMS shows that a school environment in which teachers are given autonomy can boost both teacher morale and student outcomes. Letting teachers use their professional judgement – and giving them space to develop this – has meant students are given more considered care and make better progress. The school is freed up to do this partially by having relatively minimal influence from the state, but also significantly by its very small scale. Whilst this may seem to make the OMS experience irrelevant to large comprehensives, all schools can benefit from finding ways to involve teachers in managing their own working lives and being reinvigorated by the opportunity to do their very best for every child in their care.

Martyn Steiner, Former Head of Senior School
www.oxfordmontessori.co.uk/

Case Study 4

In Scotland it is well understood that valuing teachers as professionals is key to helping schools get the best out of their students. This case study shows the different ways in which teachers contribute to school development at St Paul's RC Academy.

Encouraging teacher participation at St Paul's RC Academy, Dundee

St Paul's RC Academy provides a range of opportunities to give teachers a voice in school improvement. The head teacher and the senior leadership team use the national and local improvement plans as a basis for developing the school within the context of its local community. The key priorities, as set out in these plans, are developed in consultation with a range of stakeholders, namely pupils, parents and teachers as well as other partners.

Once the school's priorities have been established, teachers are invited to sit on working/action groups which meet on a regular basis to discuss the priorities in the plan. The chair of each group then meets with the senior leadership team to discuss, amend or adapt each group's proposals prior to implementation.

Using the national school self-evaluation framework *How Good is Our School? (4th edition)*, *HGIOS4*, any actions are then reviewed on a regular basis. Examples in this particular school include:

- Whole staff meetings: As well as a forum for informing staff of new developments, issues and opportunities, these meetings have a thematic approach based on particular areas of school improvement. Teachers work in appropriate groupings to discuss and develop processes and procedures to support the implementation and embedding within the school. Chairs of these small groups provide a note of the discussion to the leadership team.
- In-service days: Opportunities are made available during in-service days for staff to have their say on both strategic and operational issues which may be affecting them.
- Principal teacher meetings: These will have approximately 30 people in attendance and tend to be for information sharing and consultation on key issues.
- Middle management meetings: These involve the principal teachers but this time in groups of ten. The smaller group format allows for increased participation and discussion. These meetings take place three times in the course of the year and are always attended by the head and one member of the senior leadership team. These meetings are invaluable for school leaders to gain a real sense of how teachers are feeling and to ensure that their voices are heard.
- Senior leadership team meetings: These take place three times per week. Two principal teachers are invited to one of these meetings each week and have the opportunity to raise any concerns on behalf of teachers. Their role is also to act as a sounding board to gauge staff concerns or issues or to ascertain whether the timing is right to ask staff to participate in particular activities.
- Departmental attainment reviews: These take place after exam results are issued and provide teachers with an opportunity to have a dialogue around progress and improvements in performance. There are also two Curriculum Reviews.

- Meeting with teacher representatives: The head meets with a small group of representative teachers, including union representatives, twice a year to discuss teacher workload and to agree an annual Working Time Agreement. Other meetings with this group are arranged on request from the group or the head.

To secure continuous improvement in learning and teaching there are a number of opportunities built in to the school's self-evaluation calendar for teachers to have discussions around pedagogy. Themed classroom observations occur twice a year, based on themes from the HGIOS 4 framework. Once the observations are complete, a summary of findings is shared with all staff at departmental meetings. These discussions can be challenging and whilst providing an opportunity for dialogue they are also a mechanism to help improve the classroom experience for students.

Underpinning all of the mechanisms in place to provide opportunities for teachers to have their voice heard is the pervading ethos of the school. The head actively encourages all members of staff to communicate with her face-to-face if they have concerns, ideas or proposals to engage their learners more effectively. This open-door policy allows staff to feel that they are listened to and their input is valued.

Kenny McKeown, Education Officer, Dundee City Council, and Teresa Little, Head teacher, St Paul's RC Academy

http://st-pauls.ea.dundeecity.sch.uk/

Conclusion

In recognising the role that a more democratic model of education will play in creating schools which meet the needs of their communities, the time has certainly come for teachers, who are the experts on the ground, to make their voices heard. As Professor Geoff Whitty, former Director of the Institute of Education in London and now Professor for Equity in Education at the University of Newcastle, Australia, argues in an article on *Changing Modes of Teacher Professionalism*, it is important:

> to demystify professional work and forge alliances between teachers and excluded constituencies of students, parents and members of the wider community with a view to building a more democratic education system and ultimately a more open society.

The chapters that follow look at student voice and parent voice and aim to show that students and parents also have an important, albeit different, role to play, alongside teachers, in shaping their school communities.

Bibliography

Biesta, G., Priestley, M. and Robinson S. (2012) *Understanding Teacher Agency: The Importance of Relationships*. Paper presented at American Educational Research Association, Vancouver, 2012.

Bogler, R. (2001) The Influence of Leadership Style on Teacher Job Satisfaction. *Educational Administration Quarterly*, 37(5): 662–683.

Hazell, W. (2017) ATL and NUT to merge and form a new education super-union. *TES*, 22 March 2017.

House of Commons Education Committee (2017) *Recruitment and Retention of Teachers*. London: House of Commons. Available at: www.publications.parliament.uk/pa/cm201617/cmselect/cmeduc/199/199.pdf

Ingersoll, R.M. (2003) *Who Controls Teachers' Work? Power and Accountability in America's Schools*. Cambridge, MA: Harvard University Press.

Manzone, J. (2016) Factory-farmed Teachers Will Fail Our Children. *Schools Week*, 13 February 2016.

Menzies, L. et al (2015) *Why Teach?* London: Pearson.

Priestly, M., Biesta, G. and Robinson, S. (2016) *Teacher Agency: An Ecological Approach*. London: Bloomsbury.

Schleicher, A. (2011) *Building a High-Quality Teaching Profession: Lessons from around the World* Paris, OECD. Available at: www.oecd.org/edu/school/programmeforinternationalstudentassessmentpisa/buildingahigh-qualityteachingprofessionlessonsfromaroundtheworld.htm#2

Scottish Children's Parliament (2016) *School Should be a Joyful Place: Learning and school life in Scotland*. Edinburgh: Children's Parliament.

Singh, K. (2012) *Teacher Leadership: Making Your Voice Count*. Ann Arbor, Michigan: Ed Digest.

Stevenson, H. (2016) The Time is Now: Reconstructing High Quality, Democratic, Public Education. *Forum*, 58(2): 129–134.

Stevenson, H. and Gilliland, A. (2016) The Teachers' Voice: Teacher Unions at the Heart of a new Democratic Professionalism, in Evers, J. and Kneyber, R. (eds.), *Flip the System: Changing Education from the Ground Up*. London: Routledge.

Tucker, M. (2012) A Different Role for Teachers' Unions. *Education Next*, Winter 2012: 16–20.

Ward, H. (2016) Primary schools could boycott 'chaotic' Sats tests. *TES*, 26 August 2016.

Weale, S (2016) NUT and ATL vote to merge into National Education Union. *The Guardian*, 22 March 2017. Available at: www.theguardian.com/education/2017/mar/22/nut-atl-merge-national-education-union

Whitty, G. (2008) Changing Modes of Teacher Professionalism: Traditional, Managerial, Collaborative and Democratic, in B. Cunningham (ed.), *Exploring Professionalism*. Bedford Way Papers. London: Institute of Education.

Websites

Chartered College of Teaching www.collegeofteaching.org/

Education Scotland – How good is our school? https://education.gov.scot/improvement/Pages/frwk2hgios.aspx

Manifesto 15 www.manifesto15.org/en/

Teacher Agency and Curriculum Change Research www.ioe.stir.ac.uk/events/tacc.php

Welsh Education Reforms https://assemblyinbrief.wordpress.com/tag/successful-futures/

3 Student voice

Involving students as active participants in their education

How can we get children excited and enthused about learning? What can be done to make sure that young people want to go to school and can't wait for tomorrow to come? How can learning be made so interesting, so relevant and so meaningful that people want to go on doing it all their lives? This seems to be a big challenge. Whilst children in less developed countries, where access to schooling is limited, will walk miles just to get a very basic education, children in more developed nations often see school as a chore, something to be endured. Too many children say that school is boring. Too many get turned off learning at a young age.

Perhaps they should be asked. Maybe they should be involved in decisions about what they are going to learn, when and how they are going to learn it, where the learning will take place and how they will know if they have been successful. Research tells us that when young people have a say in their education, they are more engaged and better motivated. But for the most part, schools tell children what, when, where and how to learn, thereby removing from them any sense of ownership over their education.

Society wants young people to become active participants: good citizens who can make a valuable contribution. In order to do this, they need to be able to think for themselves. It is crucial therefore that children learn to make decisions and to take responsibility for those decisions – and it is best if this starts early on in life, in the classroom as well as at home.

There are a small number of democratic schools outside the state system where this happens – Summerhill is the most well known of these – but they are few and far between.

Many schools have school councils to involve children in decision-making but all too often these only give children a say on low-level matters, things that will not make a significant difference to their enjoyment of school or their experience of learning. They are allowed to take decisions on issues that are sanctioned by senior leaders, but these are not necessarily the things that really matter to them. If, on the other hand, young people are to feel committed to their education and to have a sense of agency, they should be involved in discussions about issues that will really make a difference to them.

Children's manifesto

In 2001 and again in 2011, *The Guardian* newspaper asked children to imagine their perfect school. Hundreds of children replied from all over the country, some as individuals, whilst many sent a submission from their school. There were lots of ideas, big and small, and a manifesto of these ideas was compiled in a process overseen by a panel of 12 children. Some of the suggestions would be easy to implement: others were on an altogether larger scale. But the overarching sense was that:

> They wanted their educational experience to be tailored to them. Sausage-machine schooling, with a one-size-fits-all schedule, is their biggest complaint. They don't want to do less work (although Friday afternoons off was a popular request). They just want work that enthuses and means something to them.
>
> *The Guardian*, 3 May 2011

Many children mentioned their school councils, although a common complaint was that they had no real power. By contrast, some examples were given of instances where children had wielded some influence, for example in the appointment of a new teacher.

More primary children than secondary students responded. Themes that ran through the responses from older children included wanting to see an end to same-sex schools, streaming and segregation.

Some of the recurring suggestions proposed by children were as follows:

- Lots of different sports and activities
- Calm places to go
- Music instead of bells
- Beanbags, big-enough chairs, small-enough chairs and somewhere personal to store things
- A creative and colourful environment with lots of places to display art
- Experts coming in to talk about their work
- Greater flexibility with no compulsory subjects apart from maths and English
- More art
- More time for favourite subjects
- Kind and friendly teachers: no shouting
- Being allowed to sit with friends
- Taking children's comments seriously
- Pupils of all achievements, abilities and backgrounds learning together

- Food from all over the world
- Greenhouses to grow fruit and vegetables
- Animals to care for
- iPads to work on and USB sticks to take work home
- No homework (because you would finish your work at school)
- First-aid lessons and cookery lessons
- A choice of uniform
- Fewer tests (but not no tests at all)
- A suggestion box to share your ideas

What is initially shocking about these suggestions is that, for the most part, they are entirely sensible and it is surprising that children have to ask for them at all. Shouldn't all schools be humane, inspiring and inclusive places where children feel safe and comfortable, supported and challenged? *The Guardian* acknowledged that there were also requests for chocolate fountains and popcorn stalls, but by and large, it was reported that children were thoughtful about the responses that they sent in.

According to *The Guardian*, this exercise is one of the biggest informal surveys of children's views ever carried out and they undertook to report on their findings to policymakers and opinion formers. Some years on, it is disappointing that many of these ideas are still not the norm, however easy they would be to implement.

The four different countries which make up the UK, and which all have different education systems, each have governments which have committed in different ways to listen to children and young people and it is instructive to see how this plays out across the British Isles.

Around the UK

In England, since the 2002 Education Act, schools have been legally required to consult their pupils, and when Ofsted carries out school inspections they comment on a school's success in listening to their pupils. The Children's Commissioner for England has set up a participation network and advisory groups in order to listen to young people.

In Scotland, the Children's Commissioner has commissioned research into student voice and a youth parliament has been set up. National forums and focus groups have been established to listen to children's views on different issues. Education Scotland, the national school improvement agency, has also carried out a consultation with children and young people. The *How Good Is Our School?* self-evaluation tool developed by Education Scotland encourages school leaders to consult their students when evaluating the school's progress. The Children's Parliament in Scotland has carried out a review of children's views about schools

Figure 3.1 The Joyful School
Credit: Children's Parliament, Scotland

and about learning and in 2016 released a report entitled *School Should be a Joyful Place*. Given Scotland's aspiration to be the best place in the world to go to school, the report provides much food for thought and indicates that there is still a way to go to achieve this goal.

In Wales, the School Councils Regulations 2005 require that all maintained primary, secondary and special schools in Wales must have a school council. The regulations also stipulate that school councils in secondary schools may nominate up to two council members from Years 11–13 to be associate pupil governors on the governing body. There is clearly a commitment to listening to young people's voices. However, in a recent consultation (2015–16) by the Welsh Children's Commissioner to find out children's views on a range of issues, less than 25 per cent of children said that they thought their views were listened to in schools and less than half felt that adults respected their rights. Around 80 per cent of children and young people said that they felt safe at school – but that leaves an unacceptable level of 20 per cent who don't. A Student Ambassadors scheme has subsequently been set up to listen to children's views in schools and report back to the Commissioner.

In Northern Ireland, in June 2015 the Department of Education issued a departmental circular on pupil participation in schools. This circular provided guidance for Principals and Boards of Governors on how to encourage pupil participation in decision-making and to identify ways to ensure the voice of pupils is heard. In the absence of a specific policy to ensure that children and young people are able to have a say in decisions that affect their lives within the school environment, the Northern Ireland Children and Young People's Commissioner has worked with the Northern Ireland Youth Forum to find out what young people know about participation mechanisms in their school, to discover the impact and to share best practice. The *Democra School Resource* has been produced to support this work.

In spite of all of this work on pupil participation, most schools across the UK look fairly similar to how they looked 100 years ago. It is still the case that far too few have structures or mechanisms in place that make possible a genuine and ongoing dialogue with young people about their experience of education. If they did, and if they listened, schools would in all likelihood become quite different places.

There are many different ways in which schools can encourage student participation. Broadly speaking, they fall into two main categories: student involvement in decisions about their learning – *what* they learn and *how* they learn it – and student involvement in decisions about school life. Some of these approaches are listed below:

Learning Leaders

Some schools offer training to a group of students on how to work with their teacher to support learning in the classroom. The teacher may then involve their Learning Leaders in planning the teaching and learning for their class or in developing and trialling participative approaches. Learning Leaders might also assist their teachers by, for example, organising starters or plenaries for lessons; preparing and leading a part of the lesson; and helping other students or giving feedback to teachers about their classmates' views on what helps them learn. Schools that have trained students to perform such roles and tasks have found that teachers can find it valuable to have a group of Learning Leaders to work with and consult as it helps them to better understand and meet the learning needs of their class.

See Case Study 4.

www.childreninscotland.org.uk/project/leaders-of-learning
http://my.optimus-education.com/students-learning-partners-salp

Student researchers

A number of schools have trained up a group of student researchers in different research methods, which they can then use to focus on a specific issue, gather feedback and report to senior leaders about their findings. At Mayfield School in Portsmouth, students felt that the system of rewards and punishments was unmotivational, unfair and unfit for purpose. The student research team undertook a

Figure 3.2 Leadership skills to build
Credit: Fiona Carnie

piece of work to interview and gather feedback from students, staff and parents and to investigate approaches used at other schools. Their research culminated in a proposal to the school leadership team with recommendations for changes to the school's behaviour and rewards policy. Once implemented, the new system had the support of all the main partners as everyone had felt part of the process of change.

Some primary schools are now introducing pupils-as-researchers projects and seeing a range of benefits to the children and to the school.

See Case Study 8.

http://oro.open.ac.uk/10365/

Self Managed Learning

Self Managed Learning is a structured approach to learning within which young people are able to make decisions about what and how they want to learn, how and where they plan to learn it and how they will evaluate whether they have been successful. This approach has two main elements: the learning group and the learning agreement. The learning group comprises six students of similar ages plus an adult learning adviser. The learning agreement is a contract made between the individual learner and the group which lays out the goals of the individual learner and how they will be supported by the group. This approach has been used in a number of state schools to support specific groups of students, for example 'gifted and talented' students or students at risk of exclusion.

See Case Study 6.

http://college.selfmanagedlearning.org/

Student leaders

Young people receive training in leadership, which equips them to play an active role in their school's development. Such training programmes are based on the premise that young people will do a better job in school leadership roles if they receive training in the different skills that are required. Such an approach may result in students leading on different aspects of the school's work as well as helping to nurture the leaders of the future.

See Case Study 7.

www.rsaacademies.org.uk/projects/student-leadership-programme/
www.ssatuk.co.uk/cpd/student-leadership/

Figure 3.3 Student leadership development session
Credit: Beckfoot School

Student councils

Student councils come in a range of shapes, sizes and formats. What is important is that young people can contribute to decision-making on issues which matter to them and which affect their school life and their learning. Student councils are most effective when they have the opportunity to contribute to school improvement discussions or in staff recruitment processes as such activities make a significant difference to the school and to the lives of students. Some student councils set up separate action groups so that students can focus on a particular issue. A number of schools invite the school council leaders or other senior students to attend governing body meetings so that they can report to governors and senior leaders about current issues of concern to students.

See Case Studies 1, 5 and 9.

www.schoolcouncils.org/

Student action groups

A student action group or focus group may be set up to work on one specific issue. A group of students who share an interest in the issue come together to work on it either indefinitely or for a set length of time, depending on the issue. For example, at one school, in response to a rise in bullying, a group of students work together to provide support for victims and bullies and to draw up a policy to be used by the school in an attempt to reduce the number of incidents.

See Case Studies 1, 2, 3 and 5.

www.learntolead.org.uk/
www.unicef.org.uk/rights-respecting-schools/

These are just a few examples of approaches that schools can use to encourage and support the active participation of their students. Those schools that find ways to listen to children and young people and which treat them as true partners in their education are often astonished at what can be achieved: schools where children can make real choices about their learning or what to do for homework; schools where students have an ongoing discussion with their teachers about how best they learn; schools where children teach and support each other; and schools that have children on the governing body and involve them in school decision-making.

There are many different ways of enabling students – all students, not just the most articulate, the most able and the most confident – to be active participants in rather than passive consumers of education. The following case studies showcase a range of schools and projects that give children a voice and take account of what those voices are saying. All of them exemplify schools which take young people seriously and recognise the contribution they can make to decisions which affect them. Each one demonstrates the positive impact on schools and communities when young people are consulted. They all show the extent to which young people can be a force for positive change.

CASE STUDIES

Case Study 1

Young people at The Blue School contribute to the development of their school in many different ways through their involvement in project teams, organised and led by the students themselves.

Learn to Lead at The Blue School, Wells, Somerset

Learn to Lead is a student participation framework that encourages and supports young people to contribute actively to their school community. The process starts in a school with an online survey and a whole school planning exercise so that everyone is involved from the beginning. Students identify what they perceive to be needed to improve their school. They then volunteer and 'self-elect' to form and join project teams which they manage and lead in order to develop and implement the plans they have created.

At The Blue School in Wells, a comprehensive school with 1,500 students, around 300 students are involved in all aspects of the school community and there are currently 28 teams: Africa Link, Allotment, Aquarium, Badgers and Spoons (wildlife), Beautiful School, Buddying, Dyslexia Support, Energy, Fair Trade, Finance Support, Fundraising, Garden of the Spirit, Governance Support, Healthy Living, IT Support, Kitchen Garden, Management Support, Newspaper, Office Support, Poly-tunnel, Presentations, Pond and Growing, Science Support, Shelters, Toilets, Transport, Waste and Recycling and Website.

Because students put themselves forward to set up or work on a team this approach is highly inclusive, getting away from the traditional school council model of a small elected elite which can be perceived as irrelevant and tokenistic by the majority of students. Instead, within the Learn to Lead framework, students of different strengths, abilities and ages find themselves working together, motivated by powerful self-intent. They don't just 'have a say' but they 'do', experiencing the reality of running a project. This provides young people with an opportunity to explore their own future direction, and develop a relationship of care for their community.

Community link teachers are trained and provided with tools to help them to support students to set up and run their own teams and to work in a way that encourages collaboration and mutual respect for one another. This role is integral to the approach, providing ongoing support and constant engagement with each team through regular meetings with the team facilitators. Link teachers assess when help is needed, when to direct and advise certain action and when to stand back so that the team truly experiences the responsibility they have taken on.

Once teams have formed and made plans, these are negotiated with the school management and then become part of the five-year school development plan. Students can then set to work on their plans, meeting during lunch breaks with occasional agreed time off-timetable when needed.

Every year, each team has allocated time off-timetable to attend a team review session called 'Review and Renew' where they can reflect on what went well, what could have gone better and then renew their plans for the future. The repeated process over the years releases students from the mindset of success and failure and instead helps them to learn from their past experiences and engage in a continuing journey of development.

> I used to think about school – get it over and done with. I didn't think much of it. Now I am going out of my way to help the school rather than just turn up.
>
> Secondary school student

What this approach produces is a student-run organisation with its own office at its centre, known by all members of the school community. Teams liaise constantly with different members of staff (for example, teachers, site manager, ground staff) as well as with other teams and outside organisations and businesses, giving frequent opportunities for broadening their understanding of their school and what it means to work with others.

Each team has independence and autonomy, but is aware that it is a part of the greater whole, consisting of all the teams within the school community. This 'wholeness' becomes evident at the end of each term at the gathering of all students working in project teams, called the School Forum. This is a massive circular meeting which includes members of the senior leadership team and site manager and is where everyone gets to hear what other teams have been doing. There are opportunities to raise questions, concerns and ideas and provide feedback. Cultural change has been visible in the change in dynamics in this meeting over the years at The Blue School. Students have moved from "Why don't THEY do this?" to "Why don't WE do this?" marking their sense of ownership and inclusion.

A report written by Geoff Whitty and Emma Wisby of the Institute of Education, University of London, found that:

> Amongst the more tangible outcomes of the students' work, the Transport Team completed a school travel plan as well as successfully bidding for a £12,000 grant for refurbishing the school's bike sheds ... the Toilet Team received a grant from the local authority to go towards refurbishment of the toilets. The Waste and Recycling Team arranged for two mini on-site recycling centres to be supplied by the county council. The Energy Team has launched an 'Energy Watchdog scheme', training 'Energy Watchdogs' in every tutor group to encourage both pupils and staff to remember to save energy. The Dyslexia Support Team has created a booklet to support teachers' understanding of the needs of those with dyslexia and is now trialling a system of feedback forms from pupils to teachers about each module of work. ... The Polytunnel Team and various garden teams have created a garden area. They grow vegetables which are used for school lunches or sold to staff and parents. The Learning Support department uses the garden as a resource so that their pupils can enjoy caring for a garden. ... The school council has been instrumental in encouraging fellow pupils to help the school reach the targets set by the Healthy Schools programme. ... Pupil feedback ... has been very positive: in terms of contributing to their school, the development of social and emotional skills and seeing citizenship in action. ... In practice, this provision has resulted in:
>
> - a significant proportion of pupils directly involved in the life of the school
> - a growing sense of ownership and partnership that is meaningful and non-tokenistic
> - improved relationships developing between pupils and staff based on mutual respect
> - many parents/carers appreciative of the wide range of experiences and opportunities for personal growth their children's involvement brings
> - pupils finding direction for their future and accumulating experience for future careers
> - reduced levels of vandalism, especially in areas of the school where pupils are actively involved...

This work is supported by the organisation Learn to Lead, which believes that there needs to be a shift in institutional culture to enable an approach such as this to take root. Schools are generally hierarchical and tightly structured, which leaves little space or support for student action. In this approach the power imbalance between students and staff is addressed and, where needed, teachers are given training and support to change their

attitudes towards students. An evaluation of the programme operating in 15 schools by the University of Cambridge drew attention to the fact that in the process of students developing and running their own projects, they developed a wide range of personal, learning and thinking skills.
Susan Piers Mantell, Learn to Lead
www.learntolead.org.uk

Case Study 2

Students at Sweyne Park are involved in a range of activities including pupil focus groups looking at learning and teaching, pupil panels looking at classroom practice, rights-based activities and the development of the new sixth form.

Pupil voice at Sweyne Park School, Essex

Sweyne Park School is a popular comprehensive school in Rayleigh, Essex. In 2014 it opened a sixth form in response to a strong parental and pupil-led drive to enhance the local provision of further education opportunities in the area. The school has a strong reputation partly based on its core value of respect, and this is a key characteristic in defining the organisation. The aim is for pupils and staff to be on a learning journey together, with a sense of shared vision.

One of the challenges in commenting on the impact of pupil voice at Sweyne Park from the inside is to consider what makes it different, since over time initiatives can become the new normal, possibly obscuring the aspects that might influence others wishing to develop such practices in their own establishments. In the years around 2010, Sweyne Park was at the cutting edge of pupil voice activities, with some of our pupils presenting at national conferences to share their experiences, including running pupil focus groups in parallel to the staff research and development sessions. This led to a rich debate about learning, including an exploration of thinking skills, which has continued to the present.

In 2011, driven by a couple of teachers who are passionate about the rights of young people around the world, the school became recognised as a UNICEF Rights Respecting School. Ever since, there has been a core of pupils across the range of year groups who have championed this cause. They have been inspired by the UN Convention on the Rights of a Child (UNCRC), and have consistently focused on projects to highlight the shortcomings in opportunities for many children across the world.

The fact that this initiative has for some time been led by enthusiasts and that it is totally consistent with the school's values means that furthering children's rights has become a strong part of the culture of the school and fits closely with our support of Kisarika School in Tanzania. For a number of years, teachers have been involved in staff exchanges to support teaching and learning, along with offering financial help through fundraising.

Another area key to the progression of the school is the involvement of pupil panels in meeting external consultants when carrying out subject reviews. These panels have, for many years, provided valuable information on pupil perceptions of classroom practices. Our experience has been that pupils are pleased to participate and provide constructive criticism whilst also recognising positive aspects of their education.

In 2013, one of our deputy head teachers worked closely with a Year 11 focus group, contributing significantly to the planning behind establishing the new sixth form. The purpose was to develop pupil ownership of the sixth form and to improve decision-making regarding principles such as how the sixth form would have a degree of autonomy whilst also enhancing the whole school experience. On the one hand, issues such as agreeing a dress code may seem simply pragmatic, but on the other hand, adopting a strong sense of pride in our young people through what they wear was key in setting standards. Ultimately, the group chose a uniform rather than business attire, reflecting their desire to have continuity with the rest of the school and recognising the importance of extending the school culture rather than adopting a more college-based feel. The future sixth formers were also actively involved in key appointments such as the Head of Sixth Form, which they managed with great maturity and insight. Students were also involved in thinking about what styles of teaching and learning suited them and how this could be reflected within the curriculum, in the composition of activities in the induction events. Pupil voice continues to be at the heart of the sixth form through the operation of a leadership team, subject ambassadors and a range of other groupings including a charity committee.

In sharing these ideas, it is hoped that there is no sense of having arrived at some kind of educational pinnacle around pupil voice. Such complacency is the antithesis of our culture. Rather the intention is to communicate that partnerships with our pupils and students can challenge established positions and lead to better educational solutions. Harnessing our young people's views and energies enhances our community.

Ed Hawkings, Assistant Head teacher
http://sweynepark.com/html/consultancy/pupil-voice.html

Case Study 3

ChOfsted (Children's Ofsted) was set up at Mayflower Academy to involve students in discussions about how to improve their school.

ChOfsted at Mayflower Community Academy, Plymouth

Mayflower Community Academy is for primary-aged children and is sponsored by the University of Plymouth. The Academy has developed its own bespoke curriculum which focuses on project based learning.

ChOfsted (Children's Ofsted) is a team of pupils who work in partnership with senior leaders at the Academy as well as teachers, local politicians and business leaders. The aim is to bring improvements to the school by involving students in contributing to the Academy's improvement plan. Different areas of the most current Ofsted framework are studied and dissected alongside educational reports and studies – in the context of the work of our Academy.

This is the application process:

- All Year 4, 5 and 6 pupils are invited to submit an application to become a member of ChOfsted.
- ChOfsted team members read all applications and select those who they would like to attend an interview. Interviewees are given the opportunity to deliver a presentation.
- On Interview Day, the candidates are taken on a 'learning walk' by the ChOfsted team. Following that, candidates are required to deliver a short presentation on, for example, their reflections on how the marking system helps them to become better learners.
- Applicants are then invited to come to an interview, which is conducted by the current ChOfsted team.
- Following presentations and interviews, children are provided with constructive feedback and a decision on whether they have been successful.
- Those who are unsuccessful are invited to become ChOfsted associates (advisers to the ChOfsted team).

The ChOfsted team focuses on different priorities throughout the academic year. One area of work has been the development of the Academy's marking system called PERMS, which stands for Praise, Enhance, Response, Measure and Share.

ChOfsted members are given a range of opportunities as explained below:

- Opportunities to observe a range of lessons across all year groups and conduct conversations with teachers.
- Use of social media to extend the reach of ChOfsted's pupil voice work and its impact on shaping education at the Academy as well as community development and youth culture.
- Development of oracy skills in order to present ideas articulately and fluently.
- Design and organisation of a pupil-led conference focusing on the key priorities set by ChOfsted. Presentations are made to local and national school leaders, parents and the local community, business leaders, peers and pupils from across the county.
- Development of financial understanding and how best to use the ChOfsted budget.

ChOfsted members were invited to a national leaders' conference in London in 2015 to talk about their work. One question they were asked was: If you could say one thing to all head teachers what would it be? Their answer was:

Make sure that you listen to your pupils. Sometimes head teachers are too busy and don't have the time to listen. Even if they could just spend one minute listening, that would be great!

Katie Lobb, Teacher

www.mayfloweracademy.org/pupil-leadership/chofsted

Case Study 4

Bedales students have a range of opportunities to contribute to school decision-making through their Student Teaching and Learning Group, participation in staff recruitment and regular sessions at which they are able to question the head teacher and governors.

Student voice at Bedales, Hampshire

Bedales, a liberal boarding school in Hampshire, UK, was founded in 1893 by John Haden Badley to provide an educational environment different from the strict, authoritarian options otherwise available at the time. For Badley, education was of the "head, hand and heart": a Bedales education focuses on the whole person. Bedales has been mixed, admitting girls and boys, for over 100 years. At the time, this was a pioneering step for a boarding school to take. Badley's wife, Amy Garrett, was a dedicated suffragette and early in Bedales' history, convinced her husband of the rights of girls to an equal education, challenging the prevailing consensus of the time. So Bedales has, from its inception, done things differently. The bedrock of this approach is the relationships between students and teachers, where although we have different roles and responsibilities, both are equal in importance. Central to all of this is student voice, not a new thing for Bedales: the student council is now in its 101st year. Bedales' motto is "work of each for weal of all": we strive to work collectively to achieve our educational aims.

The Bedales Student Teaching and Learning Group

The Bedales Student teaching and learning Group (STLG) is a body of students that is consulted on matters of pedagogy and curriculum policy. Any student at Bedales can volunteer their time to become a member of the group. As a result, the STLG is composed of students of all year groups, aged 13–18, and from all areas of the school: boarders and day students; girls and boys; those who consider themselves high-achievers; those who struggle more; those learning English as an additional language; and those with Specific Learning Disabilities. What these students share is an interest in excellence in teaching and learning.

The STLG is heavily involved in the recruitment of new teachers. Members form an interview panel, and with some collaborative guidance from a teacher, formulate questions, ranging from the seemingly fatuous, yet telling "if you were any cake, what type of cake would you be?" to questions about teaching style or a candidate's ideological stance on education. The student view is represented when the final decision is taken. Rarely does it transpire that the person preferred by these students is not appointed.

When discussion arises of possible new teaching and learning policy, the SLTG is a vital part of the process. The STLG might initiate discussions or might be consulted on new teaching and learning proposals. Recently there was discussion of the feedback that teachers give to students each term (our so-called 'review' cycle). The STLG felt it strange that the parents were being addressed whilst it was the students that were the subject of the feedback. Following conversation initiated by the STLG, reviews have been changed: it is now the students that are addressed. Instead of reporting that "Sarah needs to do x", the student herself is told "you need to do x". This small change makes a big difference to the tone of feedback. At Bedales, there is much invested in the teacher-student relationship, and by discussing the way that these reviews were written, the STLG brought into focus the ways in which this can be reflected and reinforced.

Another seminal change to teaching and learning policy occurred after the STLG debated the importance of self-assessment. An idea that initially came from staff, on the use of self-assessment, was strongly endorsed by the STLG. Now, the whole review cycle begins with students evaluating their progress, their effort, anything they are particularly enjoying or anything they need support with, prior to feedback given by teachers. This, coupled with the fact that reviews are now addressed to students, has made staff feedback much more responsive to specific students; part of an ongoing dialogue.

The STLG takes an active role when the whole school is consulted on matters of pedagogy or curriculum. The group trials questionnaires, comments on the appropriateness of the questions being asked and suggests additional questions. In 2015, the STLG helped prepare a questionnaire for the Harvard Research Schools International Project to be sent around to the network of some 21 schools across the globe. In this way, the group contributed not only to teaching and learning within Bedales but also within a wider international community.

Headmaster's Question Time and Governors' Question Time

The Student Teaching and Learning Group gives the school a valuable steer on matters of teaching and learning. The school as a whole, though, is engaged in questioning those running and governing the school in the termly Headmaster's and annual Governors' Question Times. Every student at the school attends these events, and any member of the community has the right to ask a question. Crucially, these questions are completely uncensored. No questions are vetted, and no one has any idea about what will be covered beforehand. Students are guided in their questioning – they need to know that a governor does not have responsibility for day-to-day operational matters at school, and that no one person should be singled out for comment, for example – but aside from those guidelines, students from the age of 13-18 may ask anything they choose about the school.

Where these events are at their best is when students hold the headmaster and the governors to the founding ethos of the school. Bedales was founded out of a commitment to a certain ethos, and our students are always keen to hold us to it. Often, we debate what exactly our ethos entails. The headmaster might be asked, for example, how a school that wants its students to achieve academically can maintain values such as "head, hand and heart" – and they will receive an honest response. Students are also keen to know how we can do better, holding those in charge to com-mitments in regard to the environment, engagement with the community or raising money for bursary places.

By consulting the STLG and holding such events as Headmaster's Question Time and Governors' Question Time, our community demonstrates an aware-ness that student voice and student flourishing go hand-in-hand. It shows both our commitment to the relationship between teacher and student and also creates in the minds of students the assumption that their views matter and will be listened to.

Sam Harding, Head Girl, and Clare Jarmy, Head of Academic Enrichment and Oxbridge and Head of Religious Studies and Philosophy
www.bedales.org.uk/

Case Study 5

Pupil voice work at Glyncollen Primary School in Wales is organised through pupil participation groups on a wide range of themes and based on the UNCRC.

Pupil voice at Glyncollen Primary School, Swansea

Pupil voice lives and breathes at Glyncollen Primary School. You will see it every day in every element of school life. Although there is a school council which exists in statute, it is an overarching body to the 'Rainbow of Responsibility', pupil participation groups which make decisions about a wide range of issues: Excellent Ecos (Sustainability), Healthy Schools, Learning Detectives, Rights Respecting Committee, Guardians (playground support group), CriwClebran (Welsh Language promotion) and Fitness Friends. We also have Super Ambassadors who work with children in other schools in Swansea in partnership with the Children's Commissioner for Wales, Sally Holland.

Groups in the Rainbow are involved in decision-making which allows for continuous improvement. The groups themselves change in response to the needs of the school and some may exist for a short period in order to complete a given task, whilst others such as the Excellent Ecos Committee remain pivotal to ensuring learner involvement in driving education for sus-tainable development forward on a daily basis.

The UNCRC is at the centre of everything we do and allows every child in the school to have a voice, knowing they will be listened to. This means that those who are not elected democratically to the Rainbow are still very comfortable in expressing themselves and in being involved in school improvement, which often leads to ventures which impact on people beyond the school. Pupil voice begins from the moment children enter the classroom with 'Class Charters' which the children draw up together and 'Check-ins', which allow them to express how they are feeling before the school day even starts. Pupil involvement takes a number of forms throughout the day, term and year. Very little happens which doesn't involve them.

One such example of the consistent approach to involving the children happened recently. We support a school in Kenya in partnership with a local college, by raising money through an annual charity walk. Staff and students from the college visited us to answer the children's questions about the school, its students and where the money goes. The Rainbow groups organised the visit from start to finish, greeting the visitors at reception, making notes on the information and preparing a presentation for the rest of the school. Our visitors commented that they had vastly underestimated what primary school children are capable of. We feel that this is a message well worth sharing in these changing times.

The development of pupil voice has contributed to the family ethos which is so tangible at Glyncollen. As such, relationships are respectful, and this has a positive impact on behaviour and engagement. The children also share their knowledge of rights beyond the school, with their parents, children and staff from other schools and government officials across Wales, including Assembly Members, sporting personalities and local organisations such as Coastal Housing. Our children are keen to ensure that all adults working with children do their best for them, according to Article 3 of the UNCRC, and will voice their opinions and ideas on issues affecting children quite readily.

As a Restorative Practice school the use of pupil voice extends into behaviour strategies, enabling children to find ways to talk about, deal with and report inappropriate behaviour. This ensures there is as little disruption as possible in their learning and also empowers them at home and in their social circles. They often use the language of rights to discuss these things such as "He was taking away my right to play", etc. Nearly all children learn to self-regulate their behaviour following discussion, learn strategies for the future and know when and how to involve adults in solving problems as they arise.

Our children know that they can and do make a difference and this is evident even in the fabric of the building. Some of our pupils took part in the Swansea Safer Routes to School initiative. Their activities in the local community, including 'walk to school' and 'keep your speed down' can be seen on the Pupil Voice Wales website as good practice. Even more importantly, they were successful in a bid which led to traffic calming around the school and a much-needed new pathway at the entrance to the school which has separated traffic from pedestrians and created a level egress for all, to create an even more inclusive environment.

It is quite usual for the children to feel empowered to make a difference for others. This includes a variety of charity ventures they will ask to hold, arrange and raise funds for. They make things to sell, hold events and provide services such as car washing. For two years running, a group of children have been recognised by the local authority in the Hi 5 Awards, given to those who are doing something to help their community. The children in Year 4 raised money for two chosen charities by making and selling items, going the extra mile for others. Younger children lobbied the Welsh government for a bin to be put outside the local shop as they were outraged at the litter problem. They were successful in their task. Similarly, older children lobbied the government to put an end to smacking.

As they grow into confident, independent thinkers, the children become more and more involved in planning their own learning. They identify resources they need or would like, especially books by authors they enjoy reading, and request them through formal letters or emails, just as they do when they have ideas for events. Similarly, they decide how to use funds raised within the school, such as the Healthy Schools committee's decision to use their funds to take out a subscription to an online fitness site which supports every class to hold a five-minute workout every day. This of course gives them a platform for practising their literacy and numeracy skills to give meaning to their learning. For some time they have given their ideas as to what themes they would like to study and how to go about it. With the school involvement in curriculum reform through the Welsh *Pioneer Schools* programme, our children are now experimenting fully with planning the themes and contexts they want to learn through. This impacts on engagement and enthusiasm and allows them to find more links in their learning as well as being involved in self-assessment and setting their own targets. The CriwClebran group has taken part in formal lesson observations throughout the school with the remit of assessing the incidental Welsh use by the children in classes. They contributed to the formal reports as part of the feedback to the teachers and reflected on the language patterns they had heard throughout the school in order to inform the Welsh Leader.

Learning Detectives have been instrumental in forming policy such as that on Homework and Effective Feedback. They have recently taken part in work for the *Pioneer Schools* programme on the vision for assessment.

Their views have been considered by a parent forum discussing the same topic before being passed to the government.

At times of crisis, even the youngest children are able to stand up and have their say as was seen when we suffered an arson attack to an outdoor playhouse. Two pupils from Reception asked if they could ring and speak to someone at the local newspaper. They gave an impassioned account of what had happened, which resulted in two local companies donating replacements when the insurance policy wouldn't cover the damage.

The assessment of pupil voice during the accreditation process for the UNICEF Rights Respecting Schools Award reported that:

> Pupils are clearly an integral part of life at Glyncollen and feel involved in all aspects of their school. There is an extensive range of opportunities given to pupils to engage with the Senior Leadership Team and contribute to decision-making in the school. All pupils interviewed reported that the school provides a range of opportunities to access information which equips them to make informed decisions.

Ultimately, all of this means that nearly all children happily negotiate, explain, take part in discussion and present to their peers and other adults, including visitors from other schools and government organisations, who often come as part of a consultation. During the run-up and the build period of the school's new extension, children were involved in choosing internal finishes and a team were part of the process from start to finish, visiting the site and reporting back to their peers.

In this way, children learn that they will be taken seriously even though the answer will sometimes have to be no. Through their involvement in the day-to-day organisation as well as long-term planning for change, the children feel valued and understand that they have a role as citizens now and for the future.

Working in this way allows vulnerable children who join our school to feel part of the school community very quickly. In the most serious cases, this can mean the difference between changing the world they live in, or accepting the status quo. When children open up to us we can involve the families and external agencies who can help bring about the change that is needed to make life better for these children.

Looking to the future, instilling the skills of pupil voice ensures that we are preparing our children for success; children who can:

- Question and enjoy problem-solving
- Communicate effectively
- Explain ideas and concepts

- Create ideas and products
- Lead and play different roles in teams effectively
- Express ideas and emotions
- Give of their energy and skills so that other people will benefit
- Use evidence in forming views and opinions
- Engage with contemporary issues
- Understand and exercise their human and democratic responsibilities and rights
- Build emotional and mental well-being by developing confidence, resilience and empathy
- Form positive relationships based on trust and mutual respect

Anna Bolt, Head teacher
https://swansea-edunet.gov.uk/en/schools/Glyncollen

Figure 3.4 Learning about our world
Credit: Glyncollen Primary School, Wales

Case Study 6

Self Managed Learning is an example of how students can take responsibility for their own learning, deciding what to learn and how to achieve their goals. The project at Uckfield Community Technology College shows how such an approach can be used to good effect within large schools. For further information about implementing this approach see Chapter 7.

Self Managed Learning at Uckfield Community Technology College, Sussex

Uckfield is a small market town in East Sussex and Uckfield Community Technology College is the only secondary school in the town. With around 1,750 students, it is bigger than many other comprehensive schools and has a large sixth form. The number of students from minority ethnic backgrounds is about average for the local authority but significantly below the national average. The level of special educational needs is above the county average, which is in turn above the national average.

The College is committed to developing a variety of approaches to learning and teaching in order to benefit all students. The personalisation agenda prompts the need to recognise that each young person is unique and worthy of a person-centred approach to his or her education. The work on Self Managed Learning, described below, was carried out by a former deputy principal before she moved on to another post.

The approach
The Self Managed Learning approach is based on students working together in learning groups of six with an adult as a learning group adviser. The students write a learning agreement specifying what they want to work on, including goals and means to achieve these. Behind this approach is the intention that students see learning as a natural process that satisfies their curiosity and enables them to accomplish the things they want to do rather than it being an imposed and passive process. Each young person is different with differing learning needs and learning preferences. Educational provision has to respond to these differences and not assume a one-size-fits-all model. In carrying out this work we had the support of a team from the University of Sussex and the Self Managed Learning Centre, led by Ian Cunningham.

The team worked with our Assistant Directors of Year (ADoYs). These full-time non-teaching colleagues worked alongside each of our Directors of Year, using and developing strategies to manage behaviour for learning; promoting positive approaches to relationships and resolving conflicts as well as pursuing attendance and other pastoral issues. This role enabled our Directors of Year to focus on supporting learning and achievement across the year groups. Ian Cunningham initially ran a workshop with our ADoYs introducing them to the approach. Each ADoY was then attached to one of Ian's team in an apprentice role so that they could develop practical experience of running groups prior to leading groups independently.

Each learning group met for about two hours every three weeks during the spring and summer terms. We started with three groups of gifted and talented students in Year 10 and followed the next year with groups from Years 8, 9 and 10. For these latter groups we identified students who would benefit from additional support. For instance, the Year 8 group was made up of boys who were in and out of short-term exclusions and who were identified as having behavioural issues in class.

Activities

Since the activities of each group were decided by the group, they varied greatly. A Year 9 group had one student who wanted to be an author. The group invited in the children's author, Jane Hissey, to question her about how she became an author and what her work entailed. Although only one student was interested in a career in this area, others in the group were able to support him by helping him come up with relevant questions to ask. As a result, others in the group learned from this experience about ways that they can explore options for themselves. One girl in the Year 9 group aspired to be a netball coach. She had the support of the group to devise questions to ask her netball coach about how he had got into coaching and what she would need to study at university.

These are examples of the group balancing independent learning with interdependent learning. Personalising cannot mean purely individualising. People have to learn how to work in real organisations with other people. This approach responds to employers' complaints that many students coming out of education are poor at team working, self-discipline and self-motivation. As well as learning what they set out in their goals, the students also developed valuable skills from the process.

This was exemplified in the Year 8 group when, in an evaluation session with students and learning group advisers, senior colleagues in the College were intrigued as to why most of the Year 8 boys had markedly improved their behaviour. The learning group adviser commented that he had not asked them to change their behaviour. They had set all their own goals and most of them had started to see a future for themselves that would require them to learn. For instance, a number were interested in becoming apprentices in motor vehicle maintenance, plumbing and electrical work.

By visiting a further education college and a local garage, they had understood the need for qualifications and what this might demand of them in the short term. This meant that they decided for themselves to take relevant lessons more seriously.

The way the group worked also provided a forum for them to take collective responsibility for behavioural issues. For instance, this group, like all others, set its own ground rules. At the same meeting they came up with a 'three strikes and you are out' rule. One boy did collect three strikes for breaking the agreed ground rules. His peers agreed that he left – and he did (for that meeting).

Given that the peer group is the biggest influence on teenagers, what we see in learning groups is the chance to mobilise the peer group for good rather than ill. We know that teachers and parents can tell teenagers not to smoke or take drugs and yet many do – through peer group influence. We cannot bury our heads in the sand and pretend this does not happen. But what we can do is create positive environments so that peer group pressure works in positive ways. The Year 8 student who was sent out of the group was shocked at getting this feedback from his peers – it's something he had never had before as normally teachers were the ones who sent him out of the class. In subsequent group meetings he was the one who most diligently policed the 'three strikes and you are out' rule.

Evaluation

The follow-up to the Self Managed Learning programme showed the value of it. For instance, some of the students from the Year 10 groups produced a list highlighting the benefits of participating in a learning group as follows:

- Thinking about our future
- Exploring further education
- Exploring career paths
- Learning from each other
- Developing our independence
- Taking more actions towards our future (not just thinking about it)
- Having a regular meeting with students and the learning group advisers to get resources/contacts to help with present problems
- Thinking about our priorities/assets/strengths/weaknesses

Teachers in Year 12 commented that students from the learning groups showed greater awareness of their future options and this had led to them being able to write their university applications more effectively.

Working in this way formed a part of our ongoing debate about the curriculum – its content and process – as well as the role of teaching and non-teaching colleagues in supporting and challenging students. Sustaining the Self Managed Learning Groups approach had implications for resources as well as basic practical considerations such as finding suitable rooms for groups to meet. It was clear, however, that this approach benefitted the students hugely.

Andrea Hazeldine, Former Deputy Principal

Case Study 7

All students at Loreto Grammar School undertake leadership training to empower them in their lives beyond school.

Student leadership training at Loreto Grammar School, Altrincham, Cheshire

Loreto Grammar School is a Catholic girls' school which focuses not only on academic achievement but on developing the whole person and preparing students for life beyond school. We have therefore been keen to promote student leadership skills. Many of our students already embrace the wide range of opportunities available at school, but we were looking to develop leadership skills in all our students in the same way that we would support the acquisition of other skills. The decision was taken that the Specialist Schools and Academies Trust's (SSAT) Student Leadership Accreditation (SLA) was appropriate for all our students in Years 7-11 to work towards with the anticipation that the different levels of accreditation would be a journey taking years rather than months.

Initially SLA was launched with staff to ensure they had a good understanding of the programme. The initiative was then presented to students in assemblies. Time was set aside at the beginning of the year to begin the creation of their leadership portfolios. Time is given during form period at points throughout the year where progress is checked and issues discussed. Students take ownership of their portfolio and their own progress, with form tutors acting as facilitators.

Our aspiration is that every student understands the importance of developing their leadership skills in preparation for life beyond school so that they can flourish in their chosen career. We expect that the majority of our students will achieve at least the Bronze award.

SLA has quickly led to an increased awareness of leadership skills. It has encouraged students to think differently about what they are doing: a geography presentation, for example, is not just a piece of homework but an opportunity for students to develop their teamwork, communication and presentation skills (three of the ten leadership skills identified by SSAT). This in turn has helped students become more reflective. It has also created another opportunity for students to feel a sense of achievement.

One outcome that we did not anticipate was the development of the role of SLA Ambassador. This role came about organically and allows the notion of 'leadership of the students, by the students, for the students' to be lived out in a tangible way. The SLA Ambassadors are students that have been accredited at a 'Gold' standard. They use their leadership expertise to support other students in the completion of their SLA portfolios. This has included the Ambassadors planning and delivering assemblies, organising a rota to support students in their form period and offering a drop-in clinic.

Our students understand that leadership is not just required of chief executives of international companies but is a skill that will help them to "grow into the fullness of life and empower them to be women of courage who are alive to the needs of humanity and committed to making a better world" (from the Loreto Vision).

Frances Green, Assistant Head teacher
www.loretogrammar.co.uk/

Case Study 8

Some schools deploy students as researchers, encouraging and supporting them to undertake a research project which can contribute to school improvement. Whilst this practice is more commonly associated with secondary schools, the following anonymised case study shows this approach being used to considerable effect with younger children.

Learning from Year 2 pupils as researchers

There have been significant developments over the past 20 years in the field of pupils as researchers relating to pupils' self-directed, empirical, social research. Most accounts of such research by children and young people in English state schools have tended to focus on projects undertaken by children aged nine and above. There are a limited number of published accounts of projects in which research has been undertaken by pupils in Years 1–4 or where pupils in Key Stage 1 have taken direct action to improve their school conditions through their own action research.

The following example is drawn from a research project which took place in a large inner-city school with a whole class of 29 pupils aged six to seven. During the Spring Term over a period of ten afternoons the pupils were introduced to an accessible version of a practical social research process. As part of this, the children chose areas they wanted to find out about through collecting data in school. They enjoyed learning important new research words. They were encouraged to be 'ethical' (not do any harm), 'sceptical' (question everything) and 'systematic' (work in a step-by-step way).

The children met and researched *Anonymouse*, a soft-toy mouse and his furry brothers and sisters who helped them learn how to be kind when collecting 'data' (information) from people by protecting their identities. The children used different methods to collect data from friends and in some cases from adults, at home and school. They thought up questions to ask people and asked these using a questionnaire or face-to-face interviews. Pupils thought about what they might find out in their research and looked carefully at their data to see what they actually found out. They worked in five teams, researching their own questions to help find out about: playing and friends; literacy, numeracy and computers; bullying; learning, science, art and PE; and about school in general including the school budget and security gates. All pupils had their research projects compiled into a book to share with others whilst some had the opportunity to present their work to their classmates. Copies of individual reports were sent home.

The pupils' skills were developed through a range of activities and resources, which enabled them to choose topics and develop their ideas and understanding as the Spring Term progressed. By the beginning of the Summer Term, pupils could draw on the previous term's work to generate ideas for further research for school improvement. This included suggesting possible methods for collecting data and evaluating the practicalities of ideas.

During the Summer Term, pupils worked in four groups to research an area of the school they would like to improve. They chose prickly school bushes, large and small outdoor play equipment and shouting at playtime. They talked with the head teacher and school council about their research and ideas. The class voted to see if one group could try to stop children shouting in each other's faces at playtime. This group invited their classmates to play games during two playtimes. They asked if the games had made people happier and found out "It stopped some people from shouting in faces but it's still happening a bit!" Whilst the scale and impact of their school improvement activity was small, it enabled the pupils to engage practically in all stages of a process of improvement.

Many pupils enjoyed the whole research journey whilst some particularly liked using dictaphones or observations to collect data. For others, it was especially rewarding and empowering to receive data back from people and experience research as a vehicle by which others took seriously the need to answer their questions. Most of the children were pleased with how their research projects went and where they were less than happy they could articulate the reasons for this and suggest improvements. Whilst many were pleased they had found out new information, for others the process of finding out was most important.

The school found that their pupils benefitted from having two opportunities to pursue their own research. By pursuing their research questions in a manageable way, pupils showed they could have the stamina to see investigations through to completion with appropriate support.

In the words of the head:

> It's engaged the children tremendously and all the ones that have been involved have gained something from it and are now more able than they used to be in some shape or form. I think also that it's brought home to staff a realisation that kids are capable of working like this.

Even with the multifarious challenges facing teachers and schools, it is still possible to find justifications for pursuing such work in a cross-curricular way. Despite concerns regarding the lack of direct inspection of participation opportunities for pupils within the current Ofsted framework, sensitively supported pupil-led research can provide rich pedagogical and participatory opportunities for pupils of all ages that can add immeasurable value to a school's provision.

Ros Brown, Independent Researcher

Case Study 9

At the Integrated College Dungannon in Northern Ireland the Chair and Vice Chair of the student council represent students on the Board of Governors, thereby ensuring that students' views are taken account of in school decision-making.

Students as governors at the Integrated College Dungannon, County Tyrone

The Integrated College Dungannon is an integrated secondary school which takes students from ages 11–18. There are many ways that students at the College can express their opinions. For all students, there is the option of becoming a member of the student council. Students in the sixth form can also apply to join the Social Action Committee or the Restorative Justice Team. In all of these groups, students have the opportunity to express their views and make a difference in the College. In addition, there are many academic and pastoral reviews carried out each year with the students where our opinions and ideas for improvement are sought.

Every year, a member from each class is nominated by the students to represent them. This year we have 23 members and we meet at least once a month. In meetings, we talk about issues that council representatives feel are affecting them and their peers and discuss ideas that could help improve the College.

The meetings are entirely run by the students. A staff coordinator is present for supervision and consultation when needed. The Chairperson initially decides on what issues to talk about and generally this consists of:

- Following up on issues from the previous meeting
- Giving feedback from Board of Governors' meetings
- Reporting on progress after the monthly meetings with the principal
- Discussing items from the student council suggestion box
- Discussing requests from the senior leadership team, e.g. regarding the review of school policies
- Reps are free to express their own views and bring up any problems
- Organising charity events

We have contributed to a number of changes at the College. Transport-related issues frequently arise, particularly concerning our school buses and we have been involved in sorting them out. The school toilets were old and not very pleasant and this was a frequent topic at student council meetings. Our concerns about hygiene and requests for new toilets were raised at governors' meetings and eventually the College was able to secure funding to have new facilities installed. The student council has had an input into the design of the sports kit and we have also been consulted on all uniform changes over the years – most recently, we secured the replacement of our burgundy jumpers with black ones which are worn more readily by all. We represent students on the canteen committee and our suggestions for improvements are usually taken on board.

A wider selection of meals is now offered and we sometimes have themed food week.

All school policies relating to pastoral care are reviewed annually by the student council and the senior leadership team asks for our suggestions for improvement. This year we are working to come up with a better and fairer reward scheme for students.

Student council representatives participate in meetings of the Board of Governors and our role is the same as that of the other governors. We contribute to discussions, give our opinions and have the same entitlement to talk as anyone else. We have to step out on certain topics that are confidential such as staff issues. There is a section in governors' meetings where the student council gives an update on what is happening in our monthly meetings.

We feel that the voice of students is extremely important and valuable to the governors and senior leadership team at Dungannon. Being a member of the student council gives us the opportunity to express our own and other students' opinions to the governors and senior leaders at governors' meetings and we feel that these are taken seriously. We are asked about our thoughts on the topics raised each month. Governors want to know how we think their decisions affect the students and the College as a whole.

There are opportunities beyond the College as well. Student council representatives recently attended a Northern Ireland Council for Children and Young People (NICCY) event where we learned about the rights we had as students and how we could express our views and opinions freely. Further, three representatives from the student council were invited to attend a NICCY event called 'The Right Way'. This allowed us to discuss different topics with Members of the Legislative Assembly (Northern Ireland's parliament). We were involved in a group discussion regarding education and found it gave us a lot more knowledge and understanding of the education system in Northern Ireland.

Aaron Graham, Arnas Irzikevicius and Lauren Flynn, Student Council Members and Student Members of the Board of Governors

www.intcollege.co.uk/

Case Study 10

The Council of Portsmouth Students was set up to give school students from across the city the opportunity to meet together and share ideas about their education with a view to contributing to school improvement.

The Council of Portsmouth Students

The Council of Portsmouth Students (CoPS) was set up in 2002 as a result of a collaboration between Portsmouth City Council, Portsmouth secondary schools and the University of Sussex. It was attended by two representatives from each secondary, Pupil Referral Unit and special school in the city. Representatives met twice a term to share ideas on how to improve their education, which they then took back to their own school councils and senior management teams for discussion and implementation. In the early days of CoPS, annual city-wide Student Voice Days, involving representatives from all the primary schools alongside the secondary representatives, were held at Portsmouth City Football Club to ensure that younger children could also have a voice in shaping their education.

I found CoPS meetings fascinating – a mix of energisers, confidence raisers and time to genuinely share ideas for making schools better places to learn and grow. As a keen drama student, I could immediately see the value of using communication and confidence skills to build strong bonds between people with a shared purpose. I was also delighted to be able to freely contribute to the group. I was not alone in experiencing the CoPS process as an opportunity for personal growth and development.

My fellow CoPS members were a genuinely mixed group of students representing all the secondary and special schools. The elected chair during my first year in CoPS was a girl in care; there were young people in wheelchairs and on the autistic spectrum as well as some of the brightest young people from across the city. Catchment area, school and ability differences vanished in a climate of shared endeavour and enjoyment.

I was a member of CoPS from 2010 and became its chair in 2012. 2012 was a difficult year for CoPS. I went into the year with my eyes wide open to possibilities but it was also the year CoPS lost funding from the local city council so my goal shifted to keeping CoPS alive. By the end of the year, I was organising and managing the forum as a director of a social enterprise – Unloc. I was 16 and needed help so I recruited my friend Ben Dowling, who was the Member of the UK Youth Parliament for Portsmouth at the time, to join me on the journey of starting a social enterprise. Unloc has grown exponentially over the years. We continue to facilitate CoPS as well as creating similar forums in neighbouring areas, spearheading youth-led enterprise education and young people's soft skills development.

We took on CoPS after ten years of operation, fully knowing that we had a lot to prove and a business model to find that would sustain and safeguard the programme for future generations. The model we developed required streamlining the process to include three larger student summits a year and sub-committee meetings known as 'action groups'. Schools were required to subscribe to the service (which ultimately they all did). This enabled us to save time from an administrative perspective, achieve economies of scale and still maintain the group's core focus of creating real action and not becoming a talking shop.

With a 15-year history and a key focus on school improvement, it is inevitable that people ask "what difference has CoPS made to improving Portsmouth schools?" CoPS is a model that is not suited to those looking for a magic student voice formula that can be cut and pasted from school to school with a single-minded focus on academic outcomes rather than process and cultural change. The CoPS story has little to offer people with this mindset.

CoPS does however have an inspiring and ongoing story to tell. A story that we believe opens doors to schools working with us at Unloc to create a highly capable, actively engaged and civic-minded generation of young people. A story that offers schools an opportunity to evidence, through their work on listening to student voice, that they are preparing young people for the opportunities, responsibilities and experiences of later life. A story that demonstrates the effectiveness of creating learning communities for the benefit of learners and educators alike.

Furthermore, the work of CoPS has rippled across the city these past 15 years, having significant impacts both big and small. As a result of CoPS, there has been a city-wide student-led mental health audit, CoPS has informed and edited the city-wide anti-bullying strategy, transformed physical learning spaces as part of a '£500 budget challenge', raised over £10,000 in one day for a common cause, lobbied government over sex education, worked on an international initiative to connect classrooms around the world, launched a young people's awards ceremony and implemented a number of school radio projects across the city, to name but a few. In addition, CoPS has grown to become a respected body that represents the views of students on boards and committees on everything from religious education to safeguarding.

The impact of CoPS goes beyond the projects that we have launched. By creating ambitious and forward-thinking young citizens, members often go on to improve their school, their local community and the city after leaving CoPS. One group of students went on to host a weekly radio show about young people's issues, another campaigned for improved play facilities in their local park including a new skatepark, one developed an affordable music festival for the city's under-18 population, some created new videos to advertise the city's top attractions to the rest of the world and others have gone on to create change in university student unions across the country.

> Ultimately, Portsmouth is better off now than it was 15 years ago and CoPS has played a pivotal role in that process. Myself, Ben and the rest of the Unloc team will continue to champion youth voice in Portsmouth and beyond. It may have started in Portsmouth 15 years ago, but the story doesn't end here.
>
> **Hayden Taylor, CEO, Unloc**
>
> www.unloc.org.uk/student-forums-case-study-the-council-of-portsmouth-students/

Conclusion

The wide range of student voice work taking place at schools across the UK demonstrates what can be achieved when young people have a sense of ownership over their learning and over their schools. Time and again, school leaders and teachers say that they have been astonished at what young people can achieve when left to their own devices or what they can contribute to discussions about their learning or in the development of new projects. Time and again, experience shows that when students are given a task they step up to the plate and exceed expectations. It would seem that it is time to stop seeing young people as half-formed human beings in constant need of adult input and instead encourage and support them to take responsibility for their world.

In order to engage and enthuse young people, we must change our view of them. As Loris Malaguzzi, the founder of the inspirational Reggio Emilia schools in northern Italy, said:

> Our image of the child is rich in potential, strong, powerful, competent and, most of all, connected to adults and other children.

What are we waiting for? Let's empower young people to become active citizens so that they can create a better future.

Bibliography

Birkett, D. (2011) The school I'd like. *The Guardian*. Available at: www.theguardian.com/education/series/the-school-i-would-like

Brown, R.M. (2016) *Enabling Year 2 Pupils to Pursue Self-directed Empirical, Social Research for School Improvement: A Case Study in Two Settings*. PhD dissertation, University of Cambridge.

Education Scotland (2015) *How Good is Our School* (4th edition). Livingston: Education Scotland www.educationscotland.gov.uk

Cagliari, P. (ed.) (2016) *Loris Malaguzzi and the Schools of Reggio Emilia*. London: Routledge.

Fielding, M. and Bragg, S. (2003) *Students as Researchers: Making a Difference*. Cambridge: Pearson Publishing.

Fullan, M. (2013) The New Pedagogy: Students and Teachers as Learning Partners. *Learning Landscapes*, 6(3): 23-29. Available at: http://michaelfullan.ca/wp-content/uploads/2013/08/Commentary-Learning-Landscapes-New-Pedagogy.pdf

Montgomery, A. and Kehoe, I. (eds) (2016) *Reimagining the Purpose of Schools and Educational Organisations*. Switzerland: Springer.

Websites

Children's Rights Alliance for England www.crae.org.uk
Citizenship Foundation www.citizenshipfoundation.org.uk/
England Children and Young People's Commissioner www.childrenscommissioner.gov.uk
English Secondary School's Association www.studentvoice.co.uk/
    Training Package for School Students www.studentvoice.co.uk/student-training
National Children's Bureau Participation Support Programme www.ncb.org.uk/participation-support-programme
Specialist Schools and Academies Trust www.ssatuk.co.uk/
    Student Leadership Accreditation www.ssatuk.co.uk/cpd/student-leadership/student-leadership-accreditation/
UK Youth Parliament www.ukyouthparliament.org.uk/

Scotland
Scottish Youth Parliament www.syp.org.uk/
Scotland Children and Young People's Commissioner www.cypcs.org.uk/
Children's Parliament, Scotland www.childrensparliament.org.uk/wp-content/uploads/School-should-be-a-joyful-place-2016.pdf

Wales
Governors Wales Student participation guidelines www.governorswales.org.uk/media/files/documents/2016-07-22/Part_4_-_Section_10.pdf
Pupil Voice Wales www.pupilvoicewales.org.uk/
Wales Children and Young People's Commissioner www.childcomwales.org.uk/
    Consultation report www.childcomwales.org.uk/publications/what-next/
Welsh government announcment of the Pioneer Schools programme http://gov.wales/about/cabinet/cabinetstatements/previous-administration/2015/pioneerschools/?lang=en

Northern Ireland
Ask First Northern Ireland Standards for Children and Young People's Participation in Public Decision Making www.ci-ni.org.uk/DatabaseDocs/nav_3175978__ask_first.pdf
Northern Ireland government guidelines on pupil participation www.education-ni.gov.uk/articles/school-councils-and-pupil-participation
Northern Ireland Children and Young People's Commissioner, *Democra School Guidance Pack* www.niccy.org/professionals-practitioners-policymakers/participation/pupils-voices-pupil-participation-in-schools/pupils-voices-guidance-pack/

4 Parent voice

Building a genuine home-school partnership

In choosing a school, what many parents look for first and foremost is a safe environment, a place where their child will feel secure and be happy. Research shows that children who feel positive about school are more likely to make progress. Children who are distressed – for whatever reason – have much greater difficulty in becoming engaged in school life and in being motivated to learn. Finding a supportive school environment is therefore a high priority for parents.

Parents also want their children to succeed so that they can go on to further education or training, find an apprenticeship or get a job. Success, usually being defined in terms of passing the tests and exams which enable young people to progress onto the next stage, doesn't however take account of children's well-being. The national curriculum, SATs (Standard Attainment Tests) and league tables were introduced in the 1980s to help parents to choose between schools on the basis of the results achieved by their students.

It is questionable whether these developments have increased parental satisfaction with the education system. Many have recognised the narrowing of education caused by the national curriculum and are aware of the pressure that children are under to pass tests. English children are some of the most tested in the world and it is increasingly clear that the focus on academic achievement has had the effect of marginalising the arts, sport, environmental activities and school trips to give more time for literacy and numeracy.

Over the past three decades, successive Westminster governments have passed legislation designed to give parents (in England) the freedom to choose which school to send their child to. Different kinds of schools such as academies and free schools – some with a curricular specialism and some connected with a specific faith – have been established to offer parents greater variety.

As far as school choice is concerned, parents can only select a particular school if there are places available, if their child is admitted and if they are able to arrange the necessary transport. Many parents have found themselves on the wrong side of this policy, unable to access the school of their choice for their child. In 2017, a third of children in London and around 30 per cent of children in Birmingham failed to get into their first-choice secondary school. As things stand, many middle-class parents move house so that they are in the catchment area for their chosen school but this option is not available for less affluent parents. And in any case, all children should be able to go to good schools.

The free school programme was designed to enable parent groups to establish new schools in areas where there was a shortage of places or where parents were unhappy with the local offer. In reality, few parent groups have taken up this opportunity and many feel that the programme is divisive.

In 2016 the parent organisation PTA UK asked members for their views on current education policy and an analysis of the responses revealed the main issues of concern to parents as:

- Concern that the well-being of children is not being properly considered: that the system and pressure within it may be risking children's happiness, confidence and health.
- Concern that the current system has taken the fun and pleasure out of learning.
- Concerns about the national curriculum and assessment framework. Parents wanted this to be reviewed by an independent commission.
- Lack of understanding about how local authorities can oversee admissions and appeals without the power to increase school places in the face of demand.
- Confusion about the role of regional schools commissioners.
- Deep concern about academisation and the possible impact on pupil referral units, small schools, rural schools and special needs schools.
- Discomfort about compulsory academisation with concerns raised about academy sponsors, their remoteness, the levels of remuneration of senior players, future ownership of public assets and accountability. Parental confidence was being undermined by reports of failing academies and even fraud by trustees.
- Lack of confidence in policymakers: the content of the 2016 White Paper and some of the messages expressed after its publication made parents feel that ministers were out of touch. They wanted those who understand education and children to be able to make a proper input to its future.
- A general feeling that the government's attitude to parent governors was misplaced and that ministers don't fully appreciate the contribution that parents make and the value they have added in the past as committed volunteers.
- A request for greater openness about the capacity of the Department for Education to be able to carry two systems (maintained and academies) and about the decrease in school budgets in real terms.

It is clear that there are wide-ranging concerns on the part of parents about the general direction of education policy. With over half of all schools in England belonging to PTA UK, the findings cannot be readily dismissed.

At the same time, research indicates that many parents experience a lack of involvement in their child's school. Reinforcing the findings of a number of recent studies, a PTA UK parent insight survey conducted in 2016 found that as many as 85 per cent of parents want more involvement. Parents want to have a say on issues which affect them but see that, more often than not, schools do not have effective mechanisms enabling them to contribute to school decision-making. On the other hand, many schools report that they struggle to engage parents.

Why this disjunction? If parental involvement is one of the most powerful school improvement levers, as indicated by the research outlined in Chapter 1, why are so many schools failing to find ways to work in partnership with parents even though it is well understood that this would help to achieve improved outcomes for children and young people?

There are many issues which affect parents and on which they would like to be consulted. One such example is school reports. Parents often feel that they do not get the information that they want in their child's report or they do not get it at a time that is useful. Reports sent out at the end of the school year, for instance, mean that children do not have a chance to respond to comments until the Autumn Term, by which time they are in a new class with a different teacher. Furthermore, reports are often couched in jargon that parents struggle to understand. Many complain that schools make too much use of drop-down menus with the effect that reports are not personal to each child. Parents' evenings are another area where there is dissatisfaction. Parents often say that they spend too much time queuing to see staff and that when they do get to see the teacher, there is inadequate time for a dialogue. Teachers may tell the parents how their child is doing but not have time to discuss what needs to happen to help the child progress. Home-school communication is also an area where there is huge frustration on the part of parents, with many saying that they don't receive important information from the school or that they get it too late. Notification of meetings and events is often given at short notice so that parents find it hard to take time off work or organise childcare.

These are just a few issues where simple changes implemented by schools in response to parental feedback could make a big difference. By asking parents for their views on what works and what doesn't, schools could often find a better way – one that would suit parents, children and the school.

Those schools which do have a high level of parental involvement are generally the more successful and this is acknowledged by Ofsted. Children whose parents are able to support them in their learning are generally the ones who do best. It is important therefore that schools find ways of collaborating with parents so that they can work together to get the best for all children. The vast majority of parents listen closely to what their children say about school, care deeply about it and, given the opportunity, could make a positive input. Inevitably, the majority of parents can only give limited time because of their work commitments, but many would be willing to help provided that what was asked of them was no more than they could reasonably offer.

At present, parents most commonly get involved to assist with school fund-raising or in the organisation of social events rather than to make an input to discussions about educational issues. Schools are getting better at informing parents about ways in which they can support their child's learning at home but such communication is often one-way. How much more effective it would be if parents and teachers were to develop a mission in common and work together to achieve it. By way of example, the former head of Dartington Primary School in Devon met with a group of parents over a period of several months to build a consensus and collaboration around education by developing a partnership between parents/carers and the school. This work resulted in the creation of a shared vision and led to the establishment of the school's parent council so that parents could be actively involved in school decision-making in an ongoing way. Thirteen years later, the school continues to involve parents in school life in a range of ways and their participation has led to many positive changes, in particular, greater parental involvement in their children's learning.

But school leaders are often wary of involving parents in discussions about the curriculum or about how the school is organised because such issues are traditionally seen as the preserve of the teaching profession. There are concerns that staff professionalism will be undermined if parents become more involved and this tends to lead to an imbalance in the home-school relationship whereby parents are expected to comply with school policies without having had much – if any – input to them.

There is also an issue around training. At workshops run by Parent Councils UK, teachers have consistently commented that they were trained to work with children, not with adults. As a consequence, many feel unprepared and lack the confidence to work more closely with parents. Some feel vulnerable, especially where the relationship between home and school has not historically been very constructive. It would seem important therefore that teacher training providers include parental engagement as a mandatory theme within initial teacher training courses and that school leaders include it as part of their school's ongoing professional development programme. All school staff, not just teachers, need to feel confident about working with parents. The RSA Academy in the West Midlands has organised training on occasions to encourage staff members (teachers, tutors, learning mentors and support staff) to explore their own roles and responsibilities in working with parents. Staff members have also received help and support in doing this work. The training included a discussion about the many different barriers that prevent parents getting involved and what the school could do to overcome those barriers.

Research and practice, both in the UK and further afield, show that schools have much to gain from involving parents more closely in discussion and decision-making on every aspect of school life. Many parents have knowledge, skills and experience which are potentially useful to schools and these are often not known about or called on. Schools can be insular places and parents who are likely to work in a wide range of professions can bring an outside perspective or fresh thinking to school issues. But few schools ask their parents or members of their local community whether there are ways in which they could offer support.

Hanwell Fields Community School in Banbury conducts a Parent and Community Skills Audit to identify parents and members of the community who are prepared to give time and expertise to support the school. Walmley Junior School in Sutton Coldfield near Birmingham conducts a similar audit of parents and grandparents. In response, these schools have received offers of help such as assistance with ICT, running after-school clubs, contributing to some curriculum projects or reading with children. At a time when schools are under great pressure and teachers are working ever-longer hours, it makes sense to enlist support from the local community, where grandparents and retired people, as well as parents, might have time to spare.

Inevitably, there are parents who keep as much distance as they can from their child's school and this can be for a variety of reasons. They may have had a negative experience of school and are reticent about getting involved with an institution at which they themselves were not successful or perhaps had a miserable time. There are many such parents. Others find it hard to engage with their child's school because of language or cultural barriers or issues of confidence and self-esteem. There may be health or transport or childcare issues which hinder parents' engagement. There are parents too who have low aspirations and who fail to see the benefits that education can bring for their child. And many schools report that mental health problems are increasingly prevalent within their parent body. The onus in all of these cases must be on the school to try to find ways of reaching out so that all parents are included and can access the support that they need.

It is crucial too for parents to understand that when they send their children to school, there is an expectation that they will work with the school in order to get the best for their child. Schools cannot educate children on their own and a lack of engagement on the part of parents is not an option. It is inevitably the case that those parents which schools have the greatest need of reaching are often the hardest to engage, but that is not a reason for not trying. In order to improve outcomes for all children, schools cannot let parents off the hook. The time when a child starts at a school is critical in this regard. Schools need to be clear about their expectations of parental participation before the child even starts

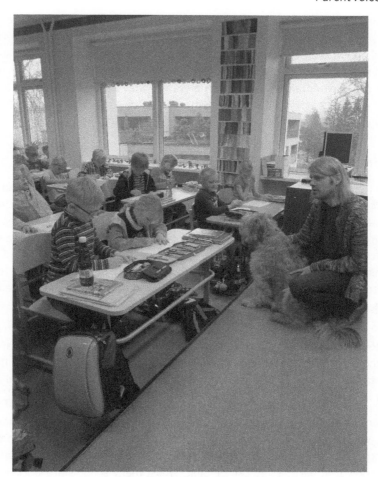

Figure 4.1 An architect father leads a lesson on how to build a kennel
Credit: Karlova School, Estonia

and must work at building that partnership from the beginning. For too long and in too many communities, the belief has existed that it is the job of schools alone to educate children.

To counter this perception, a cluster of primary schools in Sandwell worked together to develop a programme for new reception parents which covered three topics: How parents and the school can work together to support the child's learning, to encourage positive behaviour and to promote online safety. All parents were encouraged to attend these three sessions to lay the foundations for the home-school partnership.

This all raises the difficult issue of how parents can combine support for their child's education with full-time work. Parents often say that they are unable to participate in their child's school to the extent that they would wish because of the demands of their job. Until such time as society recognises the critical importance of the parental role, and government provides support for parents to fulfil it and employers are prepared to release parents to attend school events, there are limits to what can be achieved.

Parent voice

What then can schools do to establish and build this all-important partnership? How can they address some of the serious issues identified by PTA UK and referred to above? How can parents help schools resist politically motivated pressure from the government and from Ofsted and assert their right to have a say in their children's education?

Ensuring that parents have a voice in schools is surely key. As Russell Hobby, former General Secretary of the National Association of Head Teachers, said to a heads conference in 2012:

> School leaders need to leave their ivory tower and win parents over in order to wrest back control of the education system from a government that fears the voter more than it fears the strike. If we used our trust and credibility and started listening to parents about what they want and talking to them about what we can do, I think we could make a formidable team.

Research shows (see Chapter 1) that when all members of a school community work together in a genuine partnership with a shared vision and common goals, the school is strengthened immeasurably. It is important therefore to think about how that partnership can be built. Whilst many schools are working hard to engage parents in supporting their children's learning, on its own this is not enough. It is also necessary to listen to parents and work with them to shape how the school goes forward. There are two reasons for this: first and foremost, parents have the right to have a say, and secondly, the benefits that accrue to children and to schools from the involvement of their parents make the case for building parent participation.

Schools in England, Wales and Northern Ireland do, at least at present, have parent governors, but once elected, these governors are under no obligation to listen to the views of the wider parent body and reflect these back to the governing body. Furthermore, some multi-academy trusts are disbanding individual school governing bodies in favour of a trust-wide governance arrangement, making it even more difficult for parents' views to be heard. If schools are to benefit from the true engagement of parents and offer them the space in which to engage, each one must develop some kind of parent voice group so that parents can discuss and relay their views to the school leadership and governors.

The situation in Scotland is different. As part of the redesign of the education system in the early 2000s, the Scottish government introduced legislation recognising the vital part that parents play in supporting their children's learning. The Scottish Education (Parent Involvement) Act 2006 set out a new role for parents and introduced parent councils to replaced governing bodies (known as school boards in Scotland) so that parents could have a say in school decision making.

Whilst this legislation was passed ten years ago and the Scottish government has funded resources and support for this agenda through its national school improvement agency, Education Scotland and through local authorities, change has been slow in coming. Many parent councils still focus predominantly on fundraising and social events, although growing numbers are developing a closer partnership with the school in order to support student learning. At the time of writing, the 2006 Act is under review in order to agree next steps in securing parental engagement in their children's education.

There are a variety of ways in which schools can build a collaborative relationship with their parents and examples are given below. These mechanisms are needed so that from the beginning, when children start school, parents feel reassured that there are established ways in which they can communicate with the school and contribute to decisions on issues which affect them, their child and the direction of the school.

Parent councils

Parent councils enable parents to contribute to decision-making on issues which affect them and their children. Depending on the size of the school, each class or tutor group nominates a parent to represent them. For larger schools, there may be several representatives for each year group. The council, usually a group of around 10–15 parents, meets on a regular basis to discuss issues which have been put forward. There are many issues on which parents have views – for example, homework policy, class sizes, staffing, behaviour policy, uniform, home-school communication and, most importantly, the curriculum. The parent council must have a close link with the school's governing body, either through direct representation or through representatives of each body attending each other's meetings. The views of the parent body can thus be relayed to the governing body to inform school policymaking. It is also valuable for parent councils to have a link to student councils so that parents and students can work together and support each other.

Figure 4.2 Parent council at work
Credit: RSA Academy

Parent forums

As an alternative to a parent council, schools can set up a parent forum to give parents opportunities to discuss school issues and policies which affect them. Such a forum does not involve representation from individual classes or tutor groups and as such is usually more informal than a parent council. The parent forum can meet on a termly basis and any parent, carer, student, governor or teacher can attend. It can be chaired by the head teacher, the chair of governors, a parent governor, the chair of the PTA or someone else who is able to take the views of parents forward. Meetings can take many different formats and it is important that they are informal and welcoming so that all parents feel included. Small focus groups or action groups can be set up at these meetings to work on specific issues and report back to the school.

Parent class meetings

A parent class meeting is a forum for all parents of children in one class or tutor group to meet with the class teacher or tutor. There are many issues which affect all the parents of children in the same class which can be usefully discussed at such meetings. Homework, rewards and punishments, bullying, school trips, lunchtime provision and SEN support are some examples of issues about which parents frequently have questions. These meetings also provide the opportunity to address curriculum issues so that parents are clear about what is being taught, how it is taught and how they can support their child's learning at home. It is essential that parents have information about such issues so that they can share responsibility for their child's progress with the school. Parent class meetings are usually fairly informal and so are less intimidating, for some parents, than individual parent teacher consultation meetings. Furthermore, they provide teachers with an easy way to communicate with all parents at once and to build up home-school relationships.

Parent representatives

Some schools have a system of class parent representatives whereby the parents of children in one class or tutor group nominate or elect one or two representatives who undertake to liaise between home and school. This arrangement can serve as an informal and speedy way for the class teacher or tutor to contact parents or for parents to contact each other and feedback to the school.

Parent action groups

Another example of home-school collaboration is where a parent action group is set up to work on a specific issue. One example of this is an environmental action group established by parents wanting to encourage and support their child's school in working towards environmental sustainability. Parents in another school have joined forces to draw up a transport policy to reduce car use in the vicinity of the school. There is also an example of parents working together to discuss testing, which has resulted in their school finding ways to reduce the pressure on children. In yet another school, parents have joined together to improve the school playground, bringing in members of the community who have specific gardening and construction skills.

Parent focus groups

A parent focus group allows the senior leadership or governing body to find out parents' views on a specific issue such as homework or school reports or PSHE education. A single issue group is set up for one or more meeting(s) to gather parents' views on the agreed topic and is then disbanded when the task is completed. It is important that such groups include a range of parents so that different viewpoints are represented. The focus group might meet on a specified number of occasions and then report back to the school leadership or the governing body so that their views can be taken account of in school decision-making.

Parent groups and parent bodies such as those described above all offer different ways in which parents can have a voice on general policy issues at their child's school and can hold schools to account. With the demise of local authorities and the enhanced role of unelected multi-academy trusts in running schools, parent voice, in whatever form it takes, is one of the few avenues by means of which to exercise democratic accountability. Schools belong to all of us: it is through education and through schools that we shape our society for the future and this concerns us all. They are paid for out of the public purse and it is therefore only right that parental feedback – alongside the views of the other main stakeholders – should be taken into account in school decision-making. If parents think that the school is too focused on exams then the school should know. If parents think that children do not spend enough time outside or doing sport then they should have the opportunity to say this. If they think that the school's behaviour policy is too punitive then this should be discussed. If parents believe that the curriculum is too narrow, there should be a chance to review it and add their own thoughts about what and how children can learn. Clearly, parents are not all going to agree on every issue – but if there is a parent voice body, it offers a means of coming together to discuss and agree how best to go forward. Without a parent body whose job it is to gather those views, it is difficult to see how schools can meet the needs of the families they exist to serve.

There is also a strong case for democratic parent bodies at local and national level so that parents' views can be taken into account when developing policies that impact on education and which affect families. At local level, parents' views would be sought on issues that could not be resolved by individual schools on their own but over which the local authority has some jurisdiction such as special needs provision, transport and local sports and leisure facilities for young people. A local parent body could be established with representation from school parent councils.

At national level, there is also a marked absence of any democratically elected forum which can speak for parents and which can be consulted by the government on education and children's issues. Parents would surely value such a body if it could ensure that the voice of parents would be represented in any debate on national education policy. Such bodies exist in a number of other countries, ensuring that parents are consulted as a matter of course on the huge range of issues that affect families and children. Just as educational professionals and young people have little opportunity to influence education decision-making in England, parents too are locked out of this process by successive governments which have treated education as a political football rather than a public service.

CASE STUDIES

Case Study 1

Parents have a range of opportunities to make their voice heard at Quintin Kynaston school, including through the parent forum and the parent council.

Parent voice at Quintin Kynaston, London

Quintin Kynaston is a mixed, truly comprehensive and highly diverse school for 11-18 year olds with over 1,400 students, situated in St. John's Wood in the London Borough of Westminster. The school converted to academy status in 2011.

The mission statement is simple: the school aims to 'develop the best in every student'. It places a high value on both academic qualifications and whole child development and the focus is on preparing students for life, and not just for the next stage of their education. Families are recognised as an important part of the school community and staff value the partnership between home and school. They believe that when parents and teachers work together there is no limit to what can be achieved.

Parents have a voice at the school in a number of ways. The parent forum is an informal gathering of parents and carers who offer positive ideas and feedback about the day-to-day operation of the school. A fortnightly meeting takes place to provide an opportunity for effective communication between parents, teachers and other staff. These meetings take place alternately in the morning and in the evening so as to be accessible to as many parents as possible. Discussions take place on a wide range of issues and have included topics such as home–school communication; parental access to teachers; setting up a second-hand uniform shop; events for parents; queuing at lunchtime; and detention protocols. Parents can ask questions and discuss any issues of concern to them. If parents are unable to attend the forum meeting, there is a Suggestion Box in the reception area where they can post their questions.

Whereas the parent forum is open to all parents, the parent council works on a more strategic level keeping track of recurring or unresolved issues that have been raised by parents. The council works with the school to make improvements and find solutions to issues that have been raised.

The mission statement of the parent council is:

> To encourage collaboration between parents and educators to provide a vibrant learning environment for all students. To support the Quintin Kynaston vision at home and school. To nurture aspiration, resilience, and a strong community spirit in our young people in readiness for their adult life.

The parent council also meets twice each month on alternate weeks to the forum. Members of the council represent the diverse communities of the school population. Different guest speakers such as the head teacher, heads of department and other key staff or external speakers are invited to attend, depending on the agenda.

Many improvements have been made as a result of the parent council's work, including:

- Making students' schemes of work available online
- Offering curriculum workshops for parents to share information about all subjects
- Ensuring that recommended resources for different subjects are shared on the school website
- Providing contact details for heads of department on the school website for ease of communication
- Revamping the reception area so that it is more welcoming
- Requesting new signage to help organise lunchtime queues
- Welcoming parents into classrooms so that they can experience lessons
- Offering a termly award for the 'Most Communicative Department', which is chosen by the parent council.

Coral Joseph, Family Liaison Worker
www.qk.org.uk/

Case Study 2

Burlington Junior School has built up its collaborative work with parents through the establishment of a parent forum and parent class representatives.

Parent forum at Burlington Junior School, New Malden

Burlington Junior School is a four-form entry school in New Malden in London with over 60 per cent of its 450 children having English as an additional language. The school is well regarded in the local community and was rated 'good' by Ofsted in September 2014. It prides itself on providing children with a life-long love of learning.

Outreach has always been high on the school's agenda; open mornings are held on a half-termly basis on themes such as literacy, maths and science. Parents are invited in to classrooms to see teaching and learning in action. During these meetings, the school has always taken the opportunity to listen to parents' comments and suggestions, but until the parent forum was established there was never a real platform for parents to air their views. So, the Junior School decided to look into other ways of gathering parents' views. There was already a 'Change Team' at the school – consisting of parents and governors – which met at the end of Year 6 to discuss parental feedback about their experience of the school. However, this was not considered to be a large enough platform to collect vital information from a range of parents. A parent forum seemed the only way to achieve this.

The head teacher and Parent Network Leader (PNL) attended training from Parent Councils UK on how to set up a parent council or forum and then set about their mission to improve communication with parents and carers. Their aim was to create a real sense of collaboration within the school. First of all, a detailed action plan was devised, which included performance management targets in order to encourage staff to buy in to this agenda. The plan outlined the desired outcomes which ranged from greater parent attendance at curriculum open mornings to improving the number of responses on Ofsted's 'Parent View' site. A Teaching and Learning Responsibility payment was awarded as an incentive to the PNL in recognition of the importance of this work and the time commitment involved.

The first step was to have a launch event. Parents were asked what they would like the focus for this event to be and the majority chose the theme of *Science and the Great Outdoors*. Parents were then invited to a morning meeting based on this topic. Refreshments were provided and the school was delighted that 34 parents attended. During the meeting, the PNL explained the aims of the proposed parent forum and took on board the recommendations from parents. Quick wins were seen as crucial to show immediate impact from listening to parents. To this end, the school speedily implemented parents' suggestions such as sending home regular, half-termly updates of children's targets. Four years on, this is still seen as an important and useful measure.

Over the following months, a parent forum meeting was held once a term and parents' suggestions – both positive and negative – were taken on board. The meetings were led by the PNL and generally lasted around 30 minutes. Over the first year, it became apparent that meetings were better attended if parents could visit classrooms afterwards. Having refreshments at every meeting was also a must. The focus for each meeting was agreed by parents and ranged from requests for help with maths and literacy homework, to inviting in the catering provider to discuss portion sizes for older children.

Meetings generally had the same structure:

- At the beginning, the PNL would re-visit recommendations from the previous meeting and report on any actions that had been taken.
- Parents would then discuss the key theme for the meeting.
- At the end, parents would be invited to raise any questions or issues about the school. This discussion helped to shape the focus of the next meeting.

In the beginning, many parents saw the parent forum as an opportunity to push their own agendas rather than consider the good of the school as a whole. To combat this, it was reiterated that the purpose of these meetings was to celebrate the school's strong points and offer recommendations that would benefit the whole school. The feedback forms at the end of each meeting were adapted so that they included space for parents to make two positive comments about the school and one developmental comment. This approach really did help with shifting attitudes and stopped the parent forum from becoming a moaning shop. Meetings have continued in this way.

After a typical meeting, the minutes are analysed and the recommendations considered by the school's Senior Leadership Team. Action points are shared with staff and then communicated to parents through written correspondence. In the early stages, the meeting focus seemed to be on changes needed rather than recognising what the school does well. As a result, the PNL has made sure to report back at staff meetings on positive comments made by parents alongside agreed action points.

At the end of every year, Year Leaders are invited to the parent forum meeting to gather useful information about what has gone well from the perspective of parents and what could be improved for next year's parents. Some Year Leaders find this to be a rather challenging meeting. However, they have all said that it is a very useful way of gathering feedback.

As a lot of the suggestions made at parent forum meetings related to particular year groups, the decision was made to create Parent Class Representative roles. This meant that the focus in parent forum meetings could remain on topics at a whole school level. The role of the Parent Representative was to promote parent involvement in the school community through organising social events amongst parents, encouraging volunteers to help out at fundraising events and give class-specific feedback on issues arising.

Parent Representatives are valued members of the school community and the PNL meets with them every half term. Although getting parents to sign up was rather difficult at the outset, this has eased, especially since the school has been able to offer an incentive in the form of a funded after-school club for their child for a term. The school now has a Parent Representative for 14 out of 15 classes, which is a great result.

It took three years for the parent forum to become embedded in school life. It is now hard to imagine the school without it. As a result of these valuable meetings, the school has been able to adapt the service it provides, ensuring that it is a positive experience for children and their families. Ofsted (2014) has recognised some of the changes which came about because of the parent forum and in their report said that:

The school is extremely successful in engaging parents and carers with many aspects of school life, including how to help their children at home. Parents and carers are highly positive about the school. They benefit from useful assessment information which indicates how well pupils are doing and where they need to improve.

Achievements of the parent forum include the following:

- Parents suggested a change to reporting arrangements: instead of an end-of-year report they wanted a detailed report in the Spring Term.
- The school has reviewed the school's home–school communication systems and used parental feedback to tailor the way in which the school now communicates to better suit parents' needs.
- Parent forum discussions have led to changes concerning homework. Parents wanted a mixture of online and paper homework tasks, which the school now offers.
- Parents asked for more workshops about literacy. As a result, parent training has been organised to focus on practical ways in which they can support children with their spelling and grammar at home.

The parent forum has provided an excellent way to share the school's vision and development plan with the wider school community to achieve buy-in from parents and get them on board with what the school is trying to achieve.

Establishing the parent forum has been a lot of hard work and a huge learning curve. It is important for others to understand that there isn't a 'one-size-fits-all' approach and different things will work in different settings. It takes time; not all meetings will be packed to the rafters, but it is important to remain positive. The support of the head teacher is essential in ensuring that the forum can be effective by responding to parents' views.

If you go down this road, you too can create a real sense of community within your school.

Fred Williams, Year 6 Teacher and Parent Forum Leader
www.burlingtonj.kingston.sch.uk/

Case Study 3

The parent council at Devonshire Infant Academy provides a vehicle for whole school change.

Parent council and parent forum at Devonshire Infant Academy, Smethwick

Devonshire Infant Academy takes children aged three to seven and has just over 350 children on roll. The parent council was set up in 2009 and has developed into an essential part of the school. Once the first year was successfully completed the head teacher handed over responsibility for organising meetings and running parent forum meetings (for all parents) to the parent council members. Each year they grew in confidence and the meetings have provided an excellent opportunity for parents to voice ideas about how to make the school even better. Providing constructive feedback was an essential ground rule that was set early on so that the forum or council did not turn into places where parents came to have a moan but where instead staff and parents could focus on positive ways of working together. Of course, problems have been brought up but in a solution-based way and the parent council members have been very good at ensuring that this happens. The school has also been able to take ideas to the council to discuss, such as trying to engage more parents in parent workshops. Parent council members responded by being visible in the playground at the end of the school day to explain and encourage parents to get involved. Devonshire's work with parents has been praised by Ofsted and is a strength of the school. Generally, upwards of 80 per cent of parents attend events and there was a turnout of 98 per cent at one recent set of workshops for the Early Years Stage and Key Stage 1.

The school has found that a handful of key parents have stayed involved as a core group from the beginning and we have been very fortunate to have two strong parent leaders at the forefront of the council, who have also served on the governing body. They have worked closely with learning mentors, who have also been crucial in maintaining a functioning and effective parent council. These staff members have attended the meetings regularly and have provided a link with the school to enable swift and easy communication between senior leaders and parents, although parents frequently pop in to chat informally to the head about different issues and new ideas.

Perhaps the biggest change resulting from the work of the parent council has been in improving the opportunities for parents to work in partnership with the school. The council has definitely influenced this and advised on ways in which we can improve parent sessions. For example, they worked with our Special Educational Needs Leader to develop a SEN parent coffee morning. They have been clear, alongside school staff, that the best learning happens when school and home work together and we have really valued the advice and help of parent council members in developing this partnership.

The school is now at another turning point in the life of the parent council as the two key leaders are due to leave at the end of the year when their children move to secondary school. Parents and staff together are thinking about succession planning to ensure the continuity and smooth transition for the new core team. The school really values having strong parents who act as drivers for the organisation but it can mean that others depend upon them. This may mean that next year, due to the change of personnel, the school might have to step up the amount of support it gives as the team reforms and finds its sense of direction. As a legacy, the outgoing parent council leaders have organised a range of events to celebrate all things British with parents from the diverse cultures that make up the school.

Sharon Gibson, Head teacher

www.devonshireinfantacademy.org/

Case Study 4

Parents at Campie Primary School in Scotland were consulted about the development of a transition programme to meet their needs. A small action team involving parents was set up to design and implement the programme.

Consulting parents about transition at Campie Primary School, Musselburgh

In preparation for the transition of nursery children to Primary 1 (P1)* in the 2015/16 academic year, the senior management team and nursery staff approached current nursery and P1 parents and carers to help develop a new transition programme. All parents/carers were invited to attend a series of meetings to discuss how the transition programme should be developed and what should be included. The discussions focused on what parents were most concerned about, most excited about, what their children would enjoy/not enjoy and what current P1 parents/carers thought were the positive and negative aspects of the previous year's transition process.

Parental engagement in the process was very high, allowing the colla-tion of several ideas and opinions. Following the initial meetings, a smaller action team of staff and parents/carers designed a programme of events to provide a transition experience suitable for the children and for parents/carers. The programme allowed children to meet each other and their class teachers, visit their new classrooms and play in a familiar environment, visit areas in the community with their new class groups and be paired up with P7 buddies to provide all children with a point of contact outside the classroom. It also focused on including those children who did not attend the school nursery, to ensure they (and their parents/carers) felt fully inte-grated into the Campie Community.

During the transition programme, parents were invited to learn about a 'normal' school day and various sessions were run to help parents under-stand the strategies used to enable children to develop their numeracy and literacy skills.

During implementation of the programme, parents/carers were encour-aged to participate as much (or as little) as they and their children pre-ferred. Once the children were settled in, parents/carers were welcomed into the classroom environment regularly to observe what the children had been learning and were often asked to join in with a task that highlighted key learning areas. 'Soft Start' sessions were organised by each teacher and ranged from a literacy lesson with a story being read and the children being asked questions, to a small craft project that parents/carers could interact with. Some of these sessions were also just a chance to observe the children settling into their environment and for them to show their parent/carer around and explain their day. These sessions were staggered on different school days to allow as many parents/carers as possible the opportunity to attend.

Following transition to P1, the parents/carers were invited to provide feedback on the transition programme and highlight areas for improve-ment. A similar programme (with some minor alterations following feed-back) was initiated for the 2016/17 transition. The transition programme is fully supported by the management team, teaching and support staff, the parent council and the parents/carers, providing an environment where we are all involved in the process of welcoming our newest learners and par-ents to the school.

Campie Parent Council

www.edubuzz.org/campie/about-us/contact-us/

* **In Scotland, primary school classes are called P1-P7**

Conclusion

The kinds of approaches discussed in this chapter represent a cultural shift in terms of the role of parents in their children's education. One of the biggest challenges in the UK is that, unlike Scandinavia for example, it is not part of the culture for parents to be active participants in their children's school. For too long, most parents have taken their child to school and expected the school to do the educating.

The cultural juggernaut is beginning to shift, albeit slowly. Whilst many schools are stepping up their efforts to draw parents in, there is much work to be done in order to reap the benefits that accrue from educators and parents working together to get the best for children and young people. It is time to develop this partnership so that parents can support schools to provide an education that meets the needs of children and of society rather than one which is ideologically driven to support a political, neo-liberal agenda.

On his website entitled *Free School from Government Control*, Professor Michael Bassey calls on parents to wake up to the damage being done to the education system. He argues that:

> the time seems ripe for a major enquiry into state education – perhaps a commission consisting of parents, teachers' representatives, young people, academics, business leaders, eminent writers and artists, social leaders – and politicians. It could ask: What should worthwhile all-round education look like in the 21st century and how can it be achieved for all our young people?

Perhaps schools could get the ball rolling by discussing this with their parents.

It is of course recognised by educators and by parents that it is not just school that makes a difference to children's lives. Young people only spend around a quarter of their waking hours there. It is highly likely that the home environment as well as children's peer groups and the media exert a stronger influence – but school is inevitably a critical part of the mix. It is important therefore to find ways to help parents and teachers to listen to each other and work together positively and cooperatively to build a shared vision to ensure that schools and families together can provide the best possible environments for children to grow, develop, learn and flourish. Such environments can best be achieved by building from the bottom up.

Bibliography

Carnie, F. (2006) *Setting up Parent Councils: Case Study Report*. London: DfES.
Carnie, F. (2011) *Parent Participation Handbook*. London: Optimus.
Carnie, F. (2012) *Harnessing Parent Power: Training Resource for Schools*. London: Optimus.
Department for Children, Schools and Families (DCSF) (2008) *The Impact of Parental Involvement on Children's Education*. London: DCSF. Publication available at: www.education.gov.uk/publications/standard/Childrenandfamilies/Page10/DCSF-00924-2008

Epstein, J. (2010) *School, Family and Community Partnerships: Preparing Educators and Improving Schools*. Boulder, CO: Westview Press.

Hong, S. (2012) *A Cord of Three Strands: A New Approach to Parent Engagement in Schools*. Cambridge, MA: Harvard Education Press.

Ofsted (2014) *Inspection Report: Burlington Junior School*, 20–21 May 2015. Manchester: Ofsted.

Topping, A. and Marsh, S. (2017) Tens of thousands of pupils fail to get into first choice secondary. *The Guardian*, 1 March 2017. Available at: www.theguardian.com/education/2017/mar/01/national-offer-day-tens-of-thousands-of-pupils-fail-to-get-into-first-choice-secondary-school

Websites

Campaign for State Education www.campaignforstateeducation.org.uk

Briefing paper on Parents' Rights www.campaignforstateeducation.org.uk/Parents%20Rights%20-%20A%20Code%20of%20Practice.pdf

Free School from Government Control www.free-school-from-government-control.com/Wake-Up-Parents.html

Learning Wales Family and Community Engagement Toolkit http://learning.gov.wales/resources/browse-all/family-and-community-engagement-toolkit/?lang=en

National Parent Forum of Scotland www.parentforumscotland.org/

Parent Councils UK www.parentcouncils.co.uk
  Training and support for schools and parents in parent engagement and parent voice www.parentcouncils.co.uk/parentcouncils.php?P=events

PTA UK www.pta.org.uk
  Guidance on developing parent voice at your school www.pta.org.uk/Info-sheets/Developing-parent-voice-at-your-school
  PTA member survey www.pta.org.uk/News/85-per-cent-of-parents-in-England-do-want-a-say-in-education-PTA-UK-survey-reveals

Parentzone Scotland https://education.gov.scot/ParentZone?dm_i=LQE,4US9Y,JJBDEQ,ICL3J,1 PEN

Parental Engagement Network www.penetwork.co.uk
  Support for schools and settings to develop parent and community engagement http://penetwork.co.uk/welcome

Transition project and home learning project to support schools to involve parents in their children's learning http://penetwork.co.uk/funded-project/ready-for-school

RSA – Reimagining Parents' Evenings project www.thersa.org/discover/publications-and-articles/rsa-blogs/2016/10/re-imagining-parents-evening

Save the Children: Families and Schools Together www.savethechildren.org.uk/about-us/where-we-work/united-kingdom/fast

Scottish Parent Teacher Council www.sptc.info/

5 School community voice
Developing a shared vision

There are a number of schools across the UK that are doing excellent work in terms of listening to their students, their teachers and/or their parents. Various examples have been discussed in the preceding chapters. However, schools which are strong on their student voice work are not necessarily good at collaborating with their parents; schools which have worked hard to build parental involvement have not always put the same effort into student or staff engagement and those schools where teachers feel they have a real voice do not automatically value the views of their students and their parents. Furthermore, it is often the case that there is little interaction between representatives of these three groups in discussion about school policy and decision-making.

Many student councils say that they have limited opportunities to engage with their school leadership. Parent councils or parent forums may have a link with the school's governing body but often find they have no way to interact directly with teachers or students. And teaching staff are often not party to the issues which are under discussion by students or by parents. All three groups – teachers, students and parents – are often excluded from contributing to discussions and decisions which are being undertaken by school leaders and governors. And yet for those decisions to be optimal, it is important that they take account of the views of all those who will be affected. When asked, students have much to say about what helps them learn best; parents are clear about the kind of information and support they would find useful in order to support their children, and teachers know what conditions help them to be effective teachers.

Sometimes these groups will pull in different directions as the priorities for teachers, parents and students do not necessarily align. All the more reason for shared discussion and decision-making so that these differences can be discussed, addressed and moulded into school policies which can gain the support of the school community as a whole.

In building a school that meets the needs of the wider community, it is also important that local organisations and businesses and local people have an opportunity to participate and share their expertise. By discussing aspirations for the school and for local children and young people together and through a process of dialogue, negotiation and compromise, a shared understanding can slowly be developed into a common vision and a way forward that is mutually agreed. Without such a process, however challenging, it is hard to build a strong school community.

Governing bodies

In theory, a school's governing body (or in Scotland, the parent council) should be the place where the voices of these different groups come together and are considered in the round as part of the school decision-making process. But this does not appear to happen as a matter of course.

Parent governors often say that they feel like junior partners on their school's governing body, without the relevant information to make a meaningful contribution to discussions. Indeed, the parent governor role is itself under threat in England at the present time as the government endeavours to strengthen governing bodies in terms of the skill sets of their members. At the time of writing, proposals to remove the requirement of academy boards to include elected parent members are under discussion at the Department for Education.

Many teacher governors also report feeling marginalised in the governance process and that their representation on the governing body is tokenistic rather than substantive. Some governing bodies only invite teachers to attend part of their meetings, making it difficult for them to contribute as full members. And as far as students are concerned, whilst a small number of governing bodies have student governor representatives or include student voice as a standing item on their agenda, this is the exception rather than the norm. Some governors make it their business to spend time in their school during the school day, part of which may involve attendance at student council meetings, but again, this is discretionary rather than mandatory and as a consequence, student participation in school decision-making is rare.

A significant part of the problem is the often inadequate induction arrangements for new governors. It can be difficult for those joining governing bodies, be they parents, teachers or other representatives, to understand the workings of the group and this limits their ability to make a valuable contribution from the outset.

There is also a very real challenge to the democratic role that a governing body could and should rightfully play resulting from the academisation agenda. Academy sponsors now play a significant and often leading role on governing bodies, meaning that the voices of those who have on-the-ground experience of a school and its local community are further marginalised. Appointees who are co-opted onto governing bodies by academy chains are there, at least in part, to promote the interests and demands of the sponsoring organisation and this has the effect of weakening the voice of parents and the school community. Some academy chains have abolished individual school governing bodies and in their place have established an overarching governance structure to oversee a number of their schools. Whilst this results in a greater consistency of approach across the chain, it reduces the responsiveness of governing bodies to each individual school's situation and to its local community. The rapid erosion of the role of local authorities in England in favour of unelected academy sponsors which are accountable only to central government has thus undermined democratic accountability within the school system.

The greatest constraining factor of all is the lack of freedom that governors and school leaders have to respond to the views of the different stakeholder groups as a result of the government's rigid accountability framework, overseen by Ofsted. Whilst successive governments have talked about the freedoms that have been ushered in through the academies and free schools programmes, in reality, school leaders and governors often feel that they have little room for manoeuvre. So whilst many teachers have been heard to say that they cannot genuinely listen to and respect the voices of their students or their parents because they themselves have no voice, so too head teachers often feel unable to respond to the views expressed by students, parents or teachers for fear that these will compromise their ability to meet the rigorous demands of Ofsted inspectors. In some ways, it is easier not to listen than to listen and be unable to deliver. This fear has resulted in an exodus of school leaders from the profession. The extent to which it is well-founded is debatable as there are a few brave school leaders and inspirational schools which have chosen to chart a course which is very different from the norm, and have survived. Equally though there are schools which have tried to introduce new approaches and found themselves heavily criticised by inspectors.

So, whilst a school's governing body is rightfully the place where the school's values and vision are articulated and agreed by representatives of the school community and the local area, and used as a reference point for school decision-making, in practice this happens all too rarely. In the wake of the huge changes that education has undergone in the past few decades, there is a strong case for reviewing the role, functions and ways of working of governing bodies to ensure that they are responsive to the communities they exist to serve and can bring about change from the bottom up. Indeed, it should be an integral part of their modus operandi that they review, on an annual or biennial basis, the core purposes of their school, taking account of the views of all key stakeholders. Such an exercise helps to ensure that the school is meeting the current needs of the local community whilst also responding to contemporary challenges in society and preparing young people with the skills and competences they need to thrive in today's world. If it were the norm for all schools to do this on a regular basis, they would be better positioned to resist the political agenda and the whims of successive government ministers, most of whom have little or no direct experience of education either from a research or a leadership perspective. Schools, like all public services, need to be flexible in order to shape the society of the future as well as respond to its current demands. Whilst recognising the huge contribution made by thousands of governors across the country on a voluntary basis, the model of governance that obtains currently is not serving us well in terms of creating schools that are fit for a democratic society.

Where then are the schools that are bucking current trends and responding with resolve to the needs of their communities? How are they bringing together the voices of teachers, school leaders, students and parents to shape a coherent, powerful and inspiring vision of education – a vision that strengthens rather than undermines democracy?

Cooperative schools

A good place to start is with the Cooperative schools movement, the very ethos of which challenges the marketisation of the English education system and its commitment to driving up standards through competition. By contrast, Cooperative schools offer a more democratic alternative within the maintained education system.

As Danny Dorling, Professor of Geography at the University of Oxford, said in the Caroline Benn 2016 Memorial Lecture:

> We need to explain again and again why cooperation trumps competition in education. Almost any fool can be taught to achieve an A* if enough resource is thrown at them. We need children who become adults who understand that there is so much more to learning than simply achieving grades in an exam.

The Cooperative movement has a long history of involvement in education. The first Cooperative school was established in Salford in the 1830s by followers of Robert Owen. There are now around 260,0000 students at over 800 Cooperative schools across England, all seeking to put cooperative values at the heart of their organisation. These principles – of self-help, self-responsibility, democracy, equality, equity and solidarity – are reflected in their membership and governance structures as well as in their approaches to curriculum, pedagogy, staff development and community engagement.

According to the Cooperative College website:

> Young people are marginalised by the media and are often negatively perceived within society but in Cooperative schools they are taking the lead, cooperating to achieve a better future not just for themselves but for their communities and society.

Cooperative schools are accountable to a stakeholder forum, which is drawn from their members – namely, staff, students, parents and members of the local community. This commitment to democratic accountability rather than top-down bureaucratic control ensures that schools are rooted in their locality. As a consequence, Cooperative schools and academies are all unique as they make their own decisions regarding timetables, holidays, curriculum, uniform and other such matters. They also each decide how to live out their cooperative values and this can look very different in different schools. Some schools may focus more on how cooperative values relate to teaching and learning in the classroom whilst others may focus on community engagement.

Cooperative schools in England are part of a well-established international movement with schools in many countries across the globe. Passmores Academy, a Cooperative school in Essex (see Case Study 1), is a good example of how cooperative values are lived out in practice within an educational setting.

A human rights based approach

How might other schools, which are not part of the Cooperative movement, arrive at a shared vision to underpin their work? One approach is to take an international framework such as the United Nations Convention on the Rights of the Child (UNCCR) and explore how this might be applied in practice at school level. The UN Convention has been ratified by every country in the world with the exception of the USA and thus provides a set of values which are more or less universally accepted. UNICEF UK has developed a programme called Rights Respecting Schools, which takes just such an approach. With guidance and support from UNICEF, schools across the UK work towards an award which demonstrates their commitment to and integration of children's rights.

At the present time, over 4,000 primary, secondary and special needs schools are working towards the Rights Respecting Schools Award (RRSA), involving more than 1.4 million children and young people. This work is based on the principles of equality, dignity, respect, non-discrimination and participation and helps schools to put children's rights at the centre of school life. Those schools which are involved claim that the award has helped to transform the climate for learning and has improved relationships across the school community by closing the divide between adults and children through the use of a common rights-respecting language. The focus on rights ensures that children's well-being takes centre stage and that there is a focus on developing the talents and abilities of each one to their full potential. Furthermore, by learning about rights and responsibilities in a global context children are empowered to become active citizens and learners.

In order to gain recognition for their efforts, schools work through two levels, self-evaluating their progress. Many schools have found that the Rights

Figure 5.1 The school community celebrates achieving Eco School status
Credit: Glyncollen Primary School, Wales

Respecting Schools Award (RRSA) provides an overarching and cohesive framework for school development.

> The school's UNICEF Rights Respecting Award threads through the whole school. It helps develop pupils' acceptance of difference and diversity, and provides them with a strong moral compass.
>
> 2016 Ofsted report, Horndean Technology College

The Rights Respecting Schools framework is powerful because it is a whole school approach involving teachers, students and parents, working collaboratively according to a shared set of values, a shared language and a shared commitment. The same rules and expectations apply to all – adults and children – in terms of how people treat each other and this reduces the hierarchical and divided atmosphere that characterises many schools.

The Department for Children, Schools and Families (DCSF) commissioned an evaluation of the Rights Respecting Schools Award in 2010 and the research report, compiled by Judy Sebba at the University of Sussex and Carol Robinson at the University of Brighton, found that:

> The RRSA has had a profound effect on the majority of the schools involved in the programme. For some school communities, there is strong evidence

that it has been a life-changing experience. The majority of school staff were truly inspired by the RRSA. Some described it as a "momentous experience". The values provided by the RRSA have, according to the adults and young people in the evaluation, had a significant and positive influence on school ethos, relationships, inclusivity, understanding of the wider world and the well-being of the school community.

Evaluation of UNICEF UK's Rights Respecting Schools Award

Horndean Technology College in Hampshire, quoted above, is an example of a school which works hard to integrate the values underpinning the United Nations Convention on the Rights of the Child (see Case Study 2).

Restorative practices

Another approach that is being used increasingly and to considerable effect, often within schools that are signed up to the Rights Respecting Schools Award, is restorative practices. This methodology, which started off in the criminal justice system, provides a framework whereby people are held to account for any wrongdoing. Instead of (or in some cases alongside) issuing punishments such as fines or prison sentences, a restorative approach brings perpetrators face-to-face with the consequences of their actions and gives them the opportunity to make amends for the harm done. Research has indicated that offenders who go through a restorative process are less likely to re-offend.

In a school setting, restorative practices are used in place of a punitive approach to behaviour management. Instead of punishments such as detentions or the withdrawal of privileges, teachers talk to students about what they have done wrong and discuss with them what they need to do to try and put things right. Together they agree what consequences will follow from the negative behaviour, with the aim that the consequence bears some relation to the wrongdoing. There is a set format for a restorative conversation based on the following questions:

Restorative questions (for the offender)

What happened?
What were you thinking about when it happened?
What do you think about it now?
Who has been affected by your action?
How have they been affected?
What do you think needs to happen next?

Restorative questions (for the victim)

What happened?
What were you thinking about when it happened?
What have your thoughts been since?
How has this affected you and others?
What has been the hardest thing for you?
What do you think needs to happen next?

There are a number of ways in which restorative practices can be used. For example, if a child has bullied one of their classmates, it can be very effective for the two children to be brought together with their respective parents and an independent adult to discuss what has happened and how this has caused the victim and the bully as well as their families to feel. Through a carefully structured conversation, a way forward can often be found that addresses the issues that have been raised. This approach generally has a longer-lasting outcome than merely punishing the bully. It can be a salutary experience for young people to have to face up to the impact of their actions on others, including their own parents. It can be a helpful process for the victim as well as the bully. Such a process often reveals the 'bully' to have issues and problems which need to be addressed. It may become clear that they are the victims of bullying or abuse themselves and once this is known, the appropriate support can be put in place.

As another example, if a child has disrupted a class, making it difficult for the teacher to teach and for others to learn, a detention requiring the child to stay behind after school is unlikely to dissuade him or her from such behaviour in the future. On the other hand, a discussion within class time in which the disruptive child hears how his or her classmates feel about their lesson being disrupted and how it makes the teacher feel is more likely to prevent a repeat of this behaviour. Students who had thought that their behaviour was clever and amusing to their peers get quite a shock when they discover that their classmates find them tiresome and actually would like to get on with their work. A gentle reproach delivered by peers is often far more effective than admonition or punishment delivered by the teacher.

This approach works in the main because it encourages people to take responsibility for their behaviour; to reflect on what they have done and how it has affected others. As with the Rights Respecting Schools framework, it applies to all members of the school community equally so that teachers who are seen to be unfair or bullying in their dealings with students may well be invited to participate in a restorative discussion. At root, restorative practices are about developing a sense of community based on respect.

Examples of restorative practices

- Learning to talk about feelings, thoughts and attitudes in class discussions
- Dealing with minor infringements through a restorative discussion between the offender and the teacher, tutor or senior student
- Addressing negative behaviour in class using circle time discussion
- Holding a restorative conference for two students who have fallen out, or in cases of bullying
- Organising a restorative panel for serious cases in order to avoid exclusion

To be effective, a whole school commitment is required so that restorative practices become a cornerstone of how the school works at every level. It can be seen as a continuum which, at one end, is about encouraging children to think and talk about their thoughts, feelings and attitudes openly with their peers and teacher. Regular class circle time or tutor group sessions on a wide range of issues help to develop student confidence to talk and discuss. This assists in building a robust school community by moving young people on from the self-centredness that often accompanies childhood and adolescence. It encourages the development of an emotionally literate environment in which people are more open and more caring towards each other.

At the other end of the spectrum, this approach can provide a process for dealing with the most serious offences as an alternative to exclusion. A restorative panel brings together a small number of staff, senior students (who have received training) and perhaps a governor or senior leader with an offender and his or her parents to discuss what has happened and how the student might be helped to change their behaviour and make amends for their wrongdoing. In more serious cases, and particularly where the wrongdoing relates to an event beyond the school gates, a community police officer might participate on the panel.

Many schools that have adopted this approach have found it transformational by directly addressing their ethos and the quality of relationships, both of which are fundamental to the creation of a positive learning environment.

Much of what has been proposed in this chapter so far may not seem particularly controversial:

- A governing body where everyone is consulted
- A school which values cooperation over competition
- A values framework based on upholding children's rights
- A restorative approach to dealing with difficulty

Quite often though, the issue is one of degree.

It is not always a question merely of whether teachers, students and parents are consulted but whether they are involved in decisions about things that really matter to them: whether they are genuinely listened to and whether changes are made as a result of what they have said.

It may not be about whether there is a commitment to cooperation – but rather how this plays out, for example in the classroom. Is there a supportive environment where all are encouraged or is it one where the strongest swim and the weakest sink?

Everyone may say that they are committed to children's rights but is the school really doing its best to protect *all* children from harm and discrimination; to give children with mental or physical disabilities the care that they need; to ensure that children are not punished in a cruel or demeaning way; to listen to all children and take them seriously. What do the 41 rights of the UNCRC really mean for school organisation?

Many schools say that they are fair and caring in their treatment of all – but do they really take time to listen to children's problems and difficulties and help them to resolve conflict in a constructive way, whether it be with other children or with adults? To do restorative work properly takes time, something that is always in short supply in schools. Corners are forever being cut in an attempt to get through the curriculum, to prepare for the tests, to comply with regulations, to get to the end of the school day. There are also training and cost implications. For instance, those schools which have committed to introducing a whole school restorative approach have generally organised training for all of their staff and also some of their senior students.

Schools which are genuinely based on a clear set of values and which live those values out in daily life will stop a class if someone is hurt, will listen to a parent who has a genuine complaint and help to resolve it, will support a struggling teacher. These are schools which put people first: schools which are based on an ethos of care. Surely this is what we want of all our schools.

One such school is the Wroxham School in Potters Bar, a primary school which sees itself as 'a listening school' and where there is a clear focus on building positive relationships based on trust. Children, teachers and parents are all valued members of the school community and their family conferences are an example of how they work together to support children's learning (see Case Study 3).

The Keele Survey

One approach which helps schools that want to strengthen the voice and participation of their teachers, support staff, students, parents and governors in the development of policy is to use the Keele Survey, which was created by the Centre for Successful Schools at the University of Keele. This survey was set up by Sir Tim Brighouse in 1989 and has been used by thousands of schools across the country. Schools can choose to survey just one group or they can survey their whole school community to gauge responses to an extensive set of questions.

Part of the value of the survey resides in getting anonymous feedback from the different stakeholder groups as a useful measure of attitudes and progress. The schools that derive the greatest benefit are those which use the feedback they receive to drive school development: schools which look in depth at the responses and reflect on what they need to do to improve.

The survey, which is administered now by the Education Survey & Research Service (EdSRS) at the University of Keele, includes a wide range of questions under headings such as:

- The quality of the school
- Relationships
- Leadership and management
- School effectiveness
- Student attitudes

Each school has the opportunity to include its own bespoke questions if there are specific areas on which they would like feedback.

In the case of teachers, support staff and governors, all are invited to complete a questionnaire. As far as students and parents are concerned, generally a sample of each group is surveyed, although the survey can be administered to all students and parents. Once completed, EdSRS analyses the data and sends a report back to the school for each group surveyed, summarising the responses and benchmarking the data against national averages. These reports give schools a useful picture of where they are in comparison with other schools and help to identify areas of strength and weakness. Some schools repeat the surveys on a regular basis, for example biennially, to help them build up a picture concerning their progress and as a way of assessing the impact of any changes made as a result of previous surveys.

Whilst many of the national findings listed on the EdSRS website are positive, there are also some less positive ones. For instance 43 per cent of primary-aged children surveyed say that other children disturb their lessons by behaving badly; 73 per cent of secondary children say that they usually feel safe at school – meaning that over a quarter do not; and only 36 per cent of teachers surveyed agree that staff morale at their school is high. It is to be hoped that schools use the data provided by the EdSRS to identify areas for improvement and dig deep in order to address issues and challenges which are revealed. Such an approach is certainly a good starting point for change if the results genuinely lead to reflection and review by the whole school community about what needs to happen next.

One school which uses the Keele Survey to positive effect is Beckfoot School in Yorkshire (see Case Study 4).

The question remains – how can schools be organised to ensure that the different groups listen to each other, and that school developments are based on a shared response and dialogue? This is crucially important so that all the groups within a school pull together and move forward based on a common set of values. Without this, there is often a lack of understanding between different groups or even mistrust.

To illustrate the potential for disagreement or tension, it helps to look at an apparently straightforward example such as homework. Even with this, it is easy for different groups within a school to pull in different directions and for there to be disagreement within groups. Some teachers, for example, want to give lots of homework to ensure that student learning during lessons is embedded. Other teachers give less. Some parents want their children to have a lot of homework to ensure that they are making the most of their education; others may feel that homework encroaches on family life, that children have spent enough of their day learning at school and need a break in the evening. As far as students are concerned, the vast majority, though not all, want as little as possible.

Furthermore, the question is not just about the quantity of homework; it also relates to how homework is marked and whether children receive feedback for the homework that they have done. There are also many questions about what kind of home learning is most effective. Should it consist of drills and exercises so that students practise what they have learned during the day? Should it consist primarily of reading? Or should it consist of longer projects where students are given time – perhaps half a term even – to explore a subject in some depth? Should they be encouraged to involve their families in their projects? And should they have a choice of what project they do?

There are many variations and inevitably, many different perspectives. What is important though is that these different views are heard: that parents, teachers and children all have the opportunity to voice their opinions and that the resulting homework policy takes account of all these views in the context of the school's overarching aims and values. Of course, it is not possible to please everyone all the time – but if people have the chance to make their voice heard and then understand the resulting policy in terms of the range of views expressed and the decisions reached about how homework can best support learning, there will be a greater consistency across the school and there is likely to be wider support for the agreed approach. It is best if teachers, parents and students can discuss an issue together so that they can hear each other's viewpoints and question each other. It is through such dialogue that mutual understanding is built up.

Homework policy is just one area, but the same applies to most school policies. Efforts to build a cohesive and dynamic school community will be most productive if all the key stakeholders are consulted about the substantive decisions. Such a democratic approach is not necessarily easy and does not give quick outcomes, but it is more likely to result in a strong and effective organisation.

Research forum

One school which developed a process for involving all the different school groups in order to reflect on progress and to agree areas for development was Bishops Park College in Clacton in Essex. Bishops Park was a new and highly innovative school, seeking to re-invent secondary education in order to best meet the needs of its students: young people who were growing up in an area of some deprivation.

The school opened in 2002 in temporary accommodation. It moved into its purpose-built campus consisting of three small schools on one site in 2005. In terms of architecture and internal school design, the organisation of the curriculum and the approach to pedagogy, its holistic view of learning and student well-being and its relationships with parents and the local community, the school attempted to shift the grounds of traditional practice. The organising principle of the school was that learning emerged from relationships – the relationship between teacher and student and the relationship between the students themselves. Professor Michael Fielding, who co-authored a report on Bishops Park with John Elliot, makes a distinction between the pastoral tradition of education and the person-centred tradition. The former separates the curriculum from the care of the whole child; the latter sees both as inextricably linked to each other, enabling learning to emerge as part of a collaborative, negotiated process grounded in the relationship of teacher and student. He placed Bishops Park in this tradition and a main aim of the research project that he led was to tease out how this process worked.

A research forum was established at the school to ensure that developments responded to the needs and concerns of the school community as a whole. The concept was devised by a small team of researchers and funded by the Innovation Unit in 2005 as a mechanism for democratic and collaborative research. The project aimed to reflect on and contribute to developments at Bishops Park College through the active participation of students, school staff, governors, parents and the local community working alongside the researchers. The research forum is described in Case Study 5.

Sadly, the school closed in 2007 after only five years due in part to falling rolls in Essex. During its short lifetime, this innovative school inspired many from the UK and further afield. It was a model of person-centred education in which the needs of each and every child were taken seriously. Amazingly for a school in such a deprived setting, all of its students proceeded on to work, apprenticeships or further education. The school made a valuable contribution to the radical, democratic tradition of education from which many have and can continue to learn.

There are then a number of examples of schools and approaches in the UK which are based on democratic principles that take account of the views of staff, students and parents in the development of school policy. The following case studies aim to show how such principles can work in practice.

CASE STUDIES

Case Study 1

Passmores Academy is a Cooperative school which seeks to integrate the core values of self-help, self-responsibility, democracy, equality, equity and solidarity in all of its work.

Passmores Academy, Harlow, Essex

Passmores Academy in Harlow is a comprehensive school in the truest sense of the word. Our town is a predominantly white community, which some would describe as working class. Harlow was a post-war new town: a sociological experiment where a mixed coterie of individuals were intended to live side by side, the variety of housing on each estate providing a blend of professionals and tradespeople alike. In reality, 70 years on, the community has become somewhat more homogenous. With its position as the third most deprived town in Essex, with the third most unemployed residents and the largest proportion of adults who have never worked (7%), it is a town where community support and a cooperative ethos is vital. 32 per cent of housing stock is council-owned and a quarter of adults have literacy and/or numeracy issues.

Passmores Academy proudly serves this community. 50 per cent of the town's students with a statement of special educational needs come to our school. The gender split is 56:44 in favour of boys. Good teachers thrive at the school but it does not suit just anyone with a degree and a teaching certificate. Our staff body is marvellously cosmopolitan and is proud to serve our community. We hope that the fine detail of the Brexit "strategy", so wholeheartedly endorsed by the town's electorate (72 per cent in favour), does not lead to a change in our teacher diversity.

As a Cooperative Academy, our school has sought to enshrine the core cooperative principles into everything we do. Just enter the Heart Space (our main atrium) and you will be confronted with the words printed around the walls in unmissable purple ink: 'Openness', 'Honesty' etc. With the core concept of one person, one vote, we have tried to seek agreement on how we operate from the widest possible range of 'stakeholders'.

Our transition to an academy took place five years ago and, rather conveniently, coincided with a physical move of 1.3 miles as we took possession of a fantastic new building in a different part of the town. There was synchronicity between the ethos and the wonderful new vistas of the school, heralding a new beginning in a very visible sense. With this in mind, we reviewed how we communicated with our stakeholders and designed a Students' Cooperative Council and Parents' Cooperative Council to meet half-termly within a day of each other. These were chaired by the same member of the leadership team, who could introduce items for discussion and hear matters arising, and then take these to the leadership team for further consideration. We also created a Student Pedagogy Team, which I will describe slightly later on.

The councils have been responsible for some fairly momentous decisions, as well as minor changes. The first agenda item each considered was the school behaviour policy: was it fit for purpose for a Cooperative Academy? We set up a staff working party to consider the same issue and the judgement of the tri-cameral parliament was unanimous – the policy was not fit for purpose.

Using each chamber to debate what was really important meant that we could get agreement on not only the rules that we wanted, but also the reasons that they were needed. Perhaps unsurprisingly, the different interest groups wanted fairly similar things: purposeful working environments, respectful conversations, safety from bullying and hate speech and such-like. Together we drafted a brand new Relationships Charter with the essential caveat that it applied to everyone who enters the building, be they a student on their first day, a visiting parent with a burning question, a teacher at the end of a long, hard day or even a Secretary of State (they do love popping in)!

We think that the charter is a shining example of cooperation – it says what we believe in and why we believe it and also gives examples. At heart it contains five affirmative statements. A sample section begins "Passmores is a caring school", and then goes on to elucidate what that means (e.g. Passmores cares for all of its members; Passmores values safe behaviour). This gives us the strength to acid-test our judgements on issues and to evaluate our own practice "Is this a caring thing to do?" "Did I place unconditional positive regard at the heart of my actions when I spoke to that child?" "Is the person with whom I am speaking, upset?" Together we move forward and together we police the boundaries that we have all agreed. It is very democratic.

Sometimes agreement is harder to find. A first example of this is the homework policy, which proved to us the dictum "You can't please all of the people, all of the time." Students tended to be in support of homework (perhaps surprisingly), as long as it was meaningful and it was marked. Staff tended to be keen to retain homework as a key way for students to develop those self-study skills that were seen as crucial to exam success. There was less of a consensus amongst parents. Perhaps because the consultation that we ran attracted those with strong views in either direction, there was strong support for homework (almost echoing the student feedback verbatim) but also a vociferous core that argued for its abolition, seeking instead for parents to develop their own children through the many and varied extra-curricular activities already in place or simply because childhood is too short to be frittered away on proxy work. The academy, I should stress, was willing to go wherever the majority view took us. Ironically perhaps, it took us not far from where we already were, and homework persisted but with a meatier policy that insisted on more timely marking, closer links to schemes of work and with a preservation of student holiday time enshrined in print.

A second example is where we became a bit more of a traditional school in our operation. We have a rule where students are not allowed onto our upper floors during a portion of lunchtime without a pass from a member of staff. This has led to a consistent period of lobbying from the students who dislike this arrangement, which is, essentially, a hygiene-control measure. Many members of the council would portray this as a grotesque infringement of their freedom of movement and have petitioned on this basis. By reference to our Relationships Charter the academy has placed the metaphorical ball firmly back in their court: "Passmores rewards those that take responsibility for their actions". We are teaching that with democracy comes responsibility – and when the student body can move around upstairs at break-time without a single piece of litter being dropped, going upstairs during the lunch break will open up to them as a democratic right. In the days when a vote comes easily and is often taken without much consideration, we are determined to teach that such freedoms come with great responsibilities too.

Our Student Pedagogy Team is a more recent development designed around our view that the development of great learning and teaching demands an ongoing conversation. Education, as ever, is an evolving animal, not least because of recent wide-ranging structural changes to our national system. We feel that we cannot legitimately have this conversation without putting students at the centre of it. It would be like a business failing to place their customers at the heart of their decisions: unthinkable.

In practical terms, the students work alongside our leaders of teaching and learning within school to place a spotlight on what they feel is working and what isn't, pedagogy-wise. They become role models of how all students can conduct the dialogue around learning, showing how to advise a teacher that a student has struggled with a learning activity in a non-confrontational way. They are able to voice frustrations on behalf of students who feel less able to do so or less comfortable in doing so. The team includes some of the less academic members: together they puzzle through the blockages in learning identified. If the team was comprised entirely of flexible, able students it simply would not be successful in identifying the issues that is made possible by having a properly cooperative and inclusive group.

Team members fulfil a range of roles based around their different strengths, i.e. micro-teaching as a demo to test pedagogies; collecting and collating student views; giving feedback to teachers and encouraging student participation in classes where teachers are trialling new methods. The students collaborate on schemes of work, co-creating where possible and advising on fine-tuning via a range of strategies and activities.

Some students concentrate on e-pedagogy and are experts on apps for education. As a result we have tried out, and continue to use, a plethora of resources. As a rule, the team makes no pretence of expertise, although in the field of app use we have found that teachers often yield to the genuinely greater skill-levels of the students in this regard. It has been a culture shift.

Additionally, the team has led Continuing Professional Development (CPD) sessions for staff, based around the speed-dating principle: learn ten new teaching strategies in half an hour, "straight from the horse's mouth and fully endorsed by users". They have travelled to conferences to share our model and ethos and have generally received a warm reception.

The older members of our initial team have now moved on to the sixth form and have set about arranging new methods of encouraging pedagogical openness and flexibility, spreading their message with zeal to those who will listen. These are the workforce and electorate of the future and we have no doubt that their work is far from over!

Passmores has benefitted massively from our connection with the Cooperative movement. The values seep into our thinking on every decision and remind us that we are all servants of our community, "mixed up together like bees in a hive", to paraphrase and re-purpose Mr Birling's famous polemic. We gain as much from our students' and parents' voices as we do from our own and, as such, gain buy-in and a sense of investing in the future. Together we are strong.

Russell King, Assistant Principal *with thanks to Stephanie Hill and Natasha Crump.*

www.passmoresacademy.com/

Passmores' Relationship Charter can be accessed online at: www.passmoresacademy.com/uploads/asset_file/3_0_relationship-charter-2015-16.pdf

Case Study 2

Horndean Technology College puts the rights of the child at the centre of school life. UNICEF's Rights Respecting Schools Award underpins the College ethos and supports the development of a respectful and inclusive environment in which all can flourish.

Respecting rights at Horndean Technology College, Hampshire

Horndean Technology College (HTC) in Hampshire provides inclusive education for students aged 11–16 and is an integral part of the local community. The school previously had Technology status and now has a specialist provision for Autism Spectrum Disorder (ASD). Students come from a very broad demographic, predominantly white British, with low ethnic diversity and include a number from areas of high deprivation.

The College upholds the rights of every child according to the United Nations Convention on the Rights of the Child (UNCRC) and offers an atmosphere of security and stability. Every individual is valued and cared for, and each person is treated as an individual. Our students are given equal opportunities to fulfil their potential and all achievements, within and beyond the curriculum, are greatly celebrated. We understand the importance of developing well-rounded young people who can make a positive contribution to their local and global community and who are successful, happy and effective citizens. We aim to prepare young people for life in modern Britain, highlighting the importance of community values and of mutual respect.

This sense of respect runs through daily life: from examples such as opening doors for each other to students asking to take on roles such as peer mentors to help and support those more vulnerable than themselves. There is positive, respectful communication between staff, students and parents, teachers engaging with students (even simply through a smile) that they may not directly teach but who they pass in the corridor and likewise students thanking teachers at the end of lessons. Students show great pride in their College and in the efforts everyone makes to ensure all students can do well. Students and staff take care of each other and want every day at HTC to be a positive experience for all.

Students can nominate each other for a house badge, based around our house system which is linked to the Olympic values. Each half-term focuses on a specific value and student nominations acknowledge those who have upheld this value in their behaviour. Students have set up support groups, for example, focusing on mental health or the LGBT+ community. With the recent development of a specialist ASD unit on our College site, students have welcomed those with physical, hearing and learning disabilities and show great respect and understanding towards those students with specific needs. Our Performing Arts department is fully inclusive and encourages all students to become involved in the arts. Our vision is of excellence for all and we want all our young people to achieve beyond their own expectations, achieving more than they first thought possible.

The Rights Respecting Schools Award (RRSA) underpins our whole College ethos. It is a strong foundation for many of our whole school strategies and it is integral to achieving our College vision. The rights of every child as outlined in the UNCRC drive our assembly and tutor pro-gramme, ensuring young people are made aware of current affairs regarding the rights of all. Students are encouraged to form opinions regarding important issues affecting their own and others' lives. We are proud of our student voice and through our Equality and Rights Ambassadors students proactively promote children's rights, equality and fairness for all. These Ambassadors have supported the development of our whole college Equality and Rights pledge and our Respect Region community charter, which promote the key value of respect and encourage respectful behaviour beyond the school gates.

Through our work on the Rights Respecting Schools Award which involves working proactively with the LGBT+ community, we have achieved the Bronze Stonewall Award. We have three designated Respect Weeks and in collaboration with our Local Children's Partnership, our students are involved in events such as our Rights Respecting Conference and hosting talks from influential speakers such as Pumeza Mandela (Education Manager for the Mandela Foundation and great niece to Nelson Mandela).

All of our stakeholders are committed to our Rights Respecting School ethos. We work collaboratively to uphold children's rights and provide an educational experience which develops each individual student's personalities and talents to the full. Our RRSA status has contributed to our whole College community having greater awareness and demonstration of respect for others within and outside school and has supported us in developing an environment where we all can be ourselves.

Layla Funnell, Rights Respecting Schools Coordinator
www.horndeantc.hants.sch.uk/

Case Study 3

The Wroxham School is committed to a person-centred approach to learning. This approach is exemplified by their family conferences which involve the child, his or her parents and the teacher in reflecting together on the child's learning and how they can best be supported.

Family conferences at The Wroxham School, Potters Bar, Hertfordshire

The Wroxham School is a co-educational primary school that sees itself as a 'listening school'. It has developed inclusive family consultation meetings that involve children, together with their parents and teacher, in reviewing their work. These meetings take place both in the Autumn and Spring Terms. Almost all parents attend (because every effort is made to offer them a suitable time, day or evening), and there is 100 per cent attendance of pupils from Year 3 upwards. Younger pupils sometimes attend; if they are not present, the meeting is still based around the same child-centred principles. The head teacher sits in on all Year 5 and 6 conferences, and others that may be considered sensitive.

A couple of weeks before the conference, class teachers meet with children individually during class time to help them think about their learning and what things they want to share during the meeting. It is stressed that it is a valuable opportunity to reflect and that adults want to listen. They are asked to look through their work and to bring something to help illustrate what they want to say.

There are some key principles underlying the family conferences:

- Place the child at the centre of their learning and at the centre of the meeting.
- Work in partnership with the child and parents.
- Encourage the child to be intrinsically, not extrinsically, motivated.
- Focus on school learning and also what they do outside school.
- Celebrate the child's achievements.
- Make the child feel safe, important, special and supported.
- Do not judge or label the child.
- Identify what more can be done to support the child to make it easier for them to learn.
- Everyone to come out of the meeting with action points.

During each family conference, teachers help to put the child and parents at ease by creating a warm atmosphere and demonstrating that they are cared about. Body language, seating arrangements, genuine praise and humour are all used to help make it a comfortable experience. The family conferences help to build positive relationships and are felt to benefit all those involved. The child feels celebrated. They may gain a sense of release from having admitted to finding something difficult and have a greater understanding about what they need to do now. Parents come out with a better understanding of their child and how they work in school, and what they as parents can do outside of school to help. The teacher learns key points about the child and gets an insight into their home life.

Underlying school culture

The school is reflective about its work and the values that underpin it. There is a person-centred approach to learning across the school and the family conferences reflect this. The aim is to create open and friendly relationships between children and staff, and parents and staff. The school's work with children, staff and parents is based on empathy and connecting with people, not setting children against adults. The school has no exclusions and rather than labelling children that find it hard to access learning, the focus is on trying to identify what the school, parents and the child can do differently. In this vein, teachers never want to make parents feel uncomfortable about what their child has done, even if they have misbehaved.

Good relationships between parents and teachers allow parents to feel able to say what they think in the meeting and for teachers to be comfortable with what they may say. Developing positive relationships has been prioritised as a part of the way the school works, through regular communication and an open-door policy. For example, nursery staff do home visits and when dropping their children off, parents can stay as long as they like in the nursery. There is space for all parents to offer feedback on school reports, a 'bring parents to school' morning, and family learning opportunities (e.g. maths) led by children. Class blogs describe homework and showcase work carried out at school.

There is a culture of dialogue and children have genuine opportunities to say what they think about what they are learning within all classrooms. This requires respectful relationships in which teachers trust that children can talk meaningfully about their learning. Children do not say "You're boring", but they might say "Wouldn't it be a good idea if...?" Teachers involve children in planning what they would like to learn and integrate this into what needs to be covered by the curriculum. This approach starts in nursery and reception where, for example, there is mostly child-initiated play. Only 19 per cent of the day within reception is spent in adult-directed learning.

Wider student voice activities help reinforce this culture of dialogue. For example, there are weekly cross-school, mixed-age circle group meetings – rather than a school council – for making and informing school decisions. Children have occasionally run the school for a day, taking on different jobs including teaching, working in the kitchen and being on reception.

Dialogue is felt to be essential within the school as children are expected to be reflective as part of their daily learning. This culture of reflective learning, and pupils' knowledge that their views are valued, is seen as key to supporting them to participate in family conferences. The level of teacher-student trust is considered crucial and has to be worked up to before introducing the review process.

The school's emphasis is firmly on learning rather than outcomes. The language of 'levels', 'targets' and 'learning outcomes' is never used with the children. The emphasis is on self-evaluation, review and decisions about areas to work on in the future. Parents do not seem interested in results or ranking.

Other examples of reflective learning at Wroxham

- Children meet individually with their teacher during class time to discuss how they think they are doing and what they want to develop.
- Children are given choices about their learning, encouraged to challenge themselves and set their own goals. There is a lot of in-class discussion about their choices and what improvements could be made, for example: if they chose the right learning partner, or whether they selected the correct challenge.
- Children review their learning in different formats. For example, a Year 6 class have their own blog/online learning journal in which they can comment on how they think they are doing in different subject areas. And in the nursery, staff keep a photo journal of children.
- Children reflect on their work in the end-of-year report that gets sent to parents, which is a written dialogue between the pupil – who says what they have done well and found challenging – and their class teacher.

Leadership and staff support

Leadership is seen as key to developing these ways of working at Wroxham. There is a shared understanding about the values that underpin the work and these apply to everyone within the school community (children, teachers, support staff and parents). The challenge for leaders is having the professional courage to be driven by these values, remembering them in everything they do and sticking to them even in the most challenging situations.

Developing good relationships between school leaders and staff - based on mutual trust - has been central in ensuring that staff feel comfortable in a situation where children are invited to talk about their learning in front of others, including the head teacher.

The head works actively with teachers to develop a learning culture in which staff feel encouraged to try new things. This includes valuing rather than judging staff, and ensuring they have a voice and choices and the support to implement their own new ideas.

Tough leadership has been needed on the rare occasion that staff continue to work against the school values and do not want to be part of the new school culture. Much more importantly however, the school has emphasised the importance of enabling, encouraging and scaffolding staff learning. This has required winning hearts and minds over time, recognising that it takes time to build a critical mass of support, in which the majority of people are moving in the same direction.

This case study is taken from a publication on Developing Student-led Reviews by Michael Fielding and Perpetua Kirby published by the Institute of Education.

www.wroxham.herts.sch.uk

Case Study 4

Beckfoot School uses the Keele Survey to ask students, staff and parents for their views on school issues. They use the feedback from these surveys to contribute to the development of school policies.

Beckfoot School - a listening school in Bingley, Bradford

Beckfoot School is a co-educational secondary school and sixth form with academy status located in Bradford in West Yorkshire. We have 1,628 students on roll with 30.3 per cent from ethnic minority groups and 14.3 per cent with SEN support. We were graded Outstanding by Ofsted in 2014 and achieved the World Class Schools award in 2016.

Student voice and leadership
Student voice and leadership is central to everything we do at Beckfoot. As far back as 2006 when the new building project began, our students played a central role in designing every aspect of the school to give it a homely and welcoming feel. Since moving into the new building, student leadership and voice have gone from strength to strength. The Beckfoot

Student Leadership (BSL) groups have designed our positive learning strategy and our rewards system as well as playing a critical role in developing the whole school strategic vision. The BSL steering group led our successful application for World Class Schools status in November 2016 and oversees student leadership at a whole school level.

Other groups include the student ambassadors (who give tours of the school and interview prospective new staff), the Buzz group (who write, edit, photograph, produce and distribute a termly school magazine) and the SMSC group (which addresses current affairs and leads on the *Prevent* agenda.) We also have year group leaders, charity leaders, sports leaders and a student welfare group. This year we are piloting individual impact projects whereby students take on a community-based project, with the aim of ensuring greater inclusivity of student leadership across the school. Finally, student voice is monitored through regular surveys and questionnaires, such as the Keele Survey, to ensure students feel valued and listened to.

These initiatives have had a huge impact on the confidence and leadership skills of our student body. The 'buy-in' to the values and principles of the school is deeply embedded given that students know they are listened to and that they attend a school designed by students for students. The aspiration to be involved in student leadership is embedded across all years as is the idea of community involvement.

Thomas Darling, Assistant Head teacher

Parental engagement

Our aim is that all parents and families are engaged and participate in their child's learning. We involve parents actively through discussions at Consultation Evenings with teaching staff and at our Student Self Review Days where their child gives a presentation on their progress, attitude to learning and how their education is enriched at school. We also hold regular parent forum groups where, together with staff, parents devise the agenda and discuss how we can further improve their child's learning experience in and out of school. Every year group has a non-teaching Learning Leader who acts as the main point of contact for parents. Learning Leaders communicate with parents in a variety of ways - through text messages, phone calls, email, meetings and home visits. We are constantly refining our practice so that parents are treated as partners and as such, we seek ways to identify any barriers to parental engagement and then look to overcome these together. We request feedback from parents through the parent forum, through correspondence with home and through gathering parents' views (verbal and written) at different events. The Keele Survey is a valuable source of information which gives us further insight into the thoughts of our parents. Feedback from the survey has helped us to improve our systems on a range of issues including home-school communication and how we report on student progress. Parents' comments and views have triggered a number of changes which have helped us to improve parent participation. Parents know their children best: our relationship with them is paramount in ensuring students enjoy learning and succeed at Beckfoot.

   Alex Denham, Assistant Head teacher

Staff voice

A vital part of our work is taking into account staff views, not only on what we are doing, but also on how we can improve. We carry out the Keele Survey every two years. We ask questions about whether staff feel proud to work in the school, about the quality of, and climate for, learning, and also about Continuing Professional Development and the school's leadership. The results, including any additional comments, are published and we always refer to the data from the previous survey. This allows us to measure trends over time and respond appropriately.

   As part of a faculty review process, teachers in each faculty also complete a survey. Again, we ask about all aspects of student learning and the appropriateness of the curriculum as well as seeking staff views on opportunities for professional development within the faculty, performance management and the quality of leadership and management within the team. Results are always compared to previous years, whole school trends and average responses. Less formal is the termly 'two stars and a wish' process, when we simply hand out 'post-it' notes and ask all colleagues to comment on things that are going well and any aspects of work they think could be improved.

   The head teacher attends every subject meeting once across the year and has an open discussion on what works well and what could be improved. In all cases, the feedback is published, but more importantly, we always make sure that we take ideas on board where possible and respond to them. An 'open-door' policy, with all leadership team members committed to speak with staff at any time, ensures that colleagues feel able to come and talk and that an ethos of approachability and openness results in ideas, views and opinions being shared within a culture of mutual trust.

   Gill Halls, Head teacher
   www.beckfoot.org/

Figure 5.2 Students entertaining residents of a local old people's home
Credit: Beckfoot School

Case Study 5

The research forum at Bishops Park College involved staff, students, parents and governors in identifying a set of criteria and indicators to help them identify what made it a good school and to agree together which issues needed to be worked on.

Research forum at Bishops Park College, Clacton, Essex

The research forum at Bishops Park was established soon after the school opened to ensure that it met the needs and aspirations of its community. The work of the forum was overseen by a research team which received funding for this innovative approach from the Innovation Unit.

The forum consisted of 12 members: one governor, two parents, four students – two from Year 10 and two from Year 7 – and five members of school staff (including one learning mentor and one member of the senior leadership team). The dissonances that arose from such a wide range of voices and perspectives were explored respectfully by means of ongoing dialogue within the group. The forum met five times in six months – the period of time allotted to the research project.

Purpose
The purpose of the forum was to assist and guide the work of the research team in constructing a set of criteria and indicators against which the work and success or otherwise of the school would be evaluated. As part

of this process it assisted the research team in setting up four focus groups.

Focus groups

Four focus groups representing the different constituencies of the school – governors, parents, staff and students – were appointed and met once during the course of the research. Their task was to feed into the research forum the data needed to construct the criteria and indicators which would be used.

Data gathering included:

- Observations of classrooms in the light of issues coming out of the research forum meetings and explored against the agreed criteria.
- Interviews and surveys with students and two sets of interviews with staff
- Construction of a case record of the research.

Criteria and indicators

In accordance with the democratic and collaborative ethos of the school, the criteria and indicators emerged from the actual ongoing work of the school as interpreted by the different data gatherers: the researchers themselves, the research forum and the focus groups, and from discussions about them that took place in the research forum. This process reflected the approaches to learning and to young people's development and well-being that were espoused by the school and were democratically agreed upon rather than imposed. The criteria and indicators were developed from the responses to two main questions put to the research forum and the focus groups:

- What makes Bishops Park College a good school?
- What issues/problems need to be worked on?

The criteria that were agreed upon addressed seven main areas of the school's work: parent/teacher relationships; teacher/student relationships; the 'Three Schools in One' organisation; curriculum and teaching, student engagement and motivation to learn; discipline; communicating evidence of students' progress; and achievements (Assessment).

For each of the criteria, the indicators depicted an aspect of 'quality' and then looked for evidence in the associated data. For teacher/student relationships, for example, the relevant criterion – "teachers generally have positive attitudes to children" was backed up by evidence – or indicators – such as "teachers trust children to work unsupervised" and "students find it easy to talk to teachers without fear of being judged".

The criteria and indicators were presented at the Bishops Park College annual residential conference, six months after the research began. They were discussed and rated for their validity by the assembled staff and the results were then used as a means of setting out clear priorities for improvement for the next year's work, based on the views of all the main stakeholders.

Conclusions

The research forum was seen by the school as a valuable way of clarifying individual and communal values and of involving the school community as a whole in an ongoing process of development. The coming together of people of different ages and backgrounds who were prepared to listen to each other in a respectful way when engaged in a practical and purposeful activity is indicative of how an intergenerational conversation can be set up and sustained.

Professor Michael Fielding, Institute of Education, University of London

This case study is taken from a publication by John Elliot and Michael Fielding entitled, Less is More: The Development of a Schools-within-Schools Approach to Education on a Human Scale at Bishops Park College, Clacton, Essex.

Case Study 6

Antonine Primary School worked with the International Futures Forum (IFF) using their transformative innovation approach and tools to rethink school improvement. (See Chapter 7 for a description of the framework and resources.)

Transformative innovation at Antonine Primary School, Glasgow

Antonine Primary School is a local authority primary school situated on a peripheral housing estate in Glasgow. The current roll is 294. Just under 70 per cent of pupils are eligible for free school meals. Being located in an area of high deprivation, the school recently qualified for additional financial support from the Scottish government aimed at improving young people's achievements.

As part of a Glasgow initiative, the school was provided with support from a senior member of International Futures Forum. Support was provided mainly through one-to-one sessions with the head teacher and deputy head and at staff meetings. A range of analytical tools was deployed with the emphasis on IFF's *Three Horizons* model and the associated transformation tools from Executive Arts. The IFF member also worked with parents from the school's parent council.

Having experienced these tools, the head teacher saw their potential for engaging students, parents and staff, all of which are priorities in achieving school improvement. She decided to use the tools and approaches in the development of the school's next and subsequent improvement plans. She understood the power of the *Three Horizons* model in providing a strategic view of the school's present circumstances and ideal future. She also appreciated the potential of the transformation tools to engage students directly in decisions about the work and life of the school and so help them to improve their own achievements more broadly.

At a number of meetings, staff participated in a series of activities supported by the *Three Horizons Kit* and the transformation tools which had been developed by IFF. Through working with these tools, teachers gained a deeper understanding of the need for change and the typical journeys that people make when taking on board new ideas, especially related to their own professional practice. The tool that was deployed to help develop that deeper understanding is known as *TransforMap*. A series of suggestions for change emerged from discussions with students, staff and parents which metamorphosed into strategic actions for the school's improvement plan.

In the period before being introduced to the various processes and tools, the school had undertaken a review of its vision, values and aims. Through engaging with the transformation tools, the school community reviewed and updated its values and aims to ensure that they embraced a vision of its ideal future. The school's values are expressed in the capacities of its 'five superheroes'. These values were referred to continually when making decisions about future priorities for action.

As a consequence of this work, the school radically altered its approach to school improvement planning. It replaced most of its extensive lists and grids of actions for improvement with a future 'map' based on the *Three Horizons*. This map included a set of actions which involved transforming how the school worked, decommissioning non-productive activities and reducing workload in order to enhance successful existing activities and map its ideal future.

One of the tools used is known as *Implemento*. It helps with identifying risks and recovery actions, stretching thinking beyond the obvious, developing a set of readily measurable outcomes and targets, and producing a pragmatic and actionable 'do list' – all in a very short space of time.

One of the priorities that the school had agreed to take on board was related to becoming an accredited Rights Respecting School (RRS).Teachers worked with children using the *Implemento* tool to plan their approach to implementing the RRS approaches. The children approached the planning tool with enthusiasm and insight. The school also applied the communication tool *Impacto*, a narrative structure designed to enrol others and secure commitment, in order to convey the important messages about the project. Because of the combined efforts of students and teachers in implementing their plan, Antonine Primary School was awarded a Level 1 RRS Award and was amongst the first schools in Glasgow to do so. The RRS assessors were impressed by the school's use of *Impacto* and *Implemento* in relation to the children's rights project.

Overall, the *Three Horizons* approach and the transformation tools have enabled the school to make a step change in its engagement of stakeholders and its improvement planning processes with considerable success.

Wendy Cameron, Head teacher
www.antonineprimaryschool.co.uk
www.internationalfuturesforum.com
www.executivearts.co.uk

Conclusion

The schools and approaches explored in this chapter all exemplify ways of working which aim to make the school the locus of control, where a sense of autonomy has been retained. All have, in one way or another, shown courage by sticking to their principles and in demonstrating these to Ofsted (or other inspection agency). This is critically important in the drive to place educational decision-making firmly in the hands of the professionals, working in partnership with their local communities. As shown in each case study, it is about developing an ethos of trust so that teachers, parents and students can work together for the benefit of students and their communities. It is about creating the space for schools to be able to respond to the needs of those they exist to serve. Politicians and civil servants are too remote to begin to be able to do this effectively. A one-size-fits-all approach to education can never be the answer. Hopefully, these examples can inspire others by showing that when schools are more democratic they are better able to serve the needs of society now and for the future.

Bibliography

Dorling, D. (2016) Let's go back to the future with cooperative schools and leave grammars in the past. *The Guardian*, 15 November 2016. Available at: www.theguardian.com/education/2016/nov/15/cooperative-schools-grammar-education

Fielding, M. and Elliot, J. (2006) *Less is More: The Development of a Schools-within-Schools Approach to Education on a Human Scale at Bishops Park College, Clacton, Essex.* Brighton: University of Sussex.

Fielding, M. and Kirby, P. (2009) *Developing Student-led Reviews: An Exploration of Innovative Practice in Primary, Secondary and Special Schools.* London: Institute of Education.

Sebba, J. and Robinson, C. (2010) *Evaluation of UNICEF UK's Rights Respecting Schools Award: Final Report to the DCSF.* Brighton: University of Sussex and University of Brighton. www.educ.cam.ac.uk/research/projects/restorativeapproaches/RA-in-the-UK.pdf

Websites

Cambridge University Research Project www.educ.cam.ac.uk/research/projects/restorative-approaches/RA-in-the-UK.pdf

Cooperative College www.co-op.ac.uk/our-work/schools-and-young-people/

Education Survey & Research Service www.edsrs.org.uk/home.html

Human Scale Education www.hse.org.uk

International Institute for Restorative Practices www.iirp.org/uk

National Governance Association www.nga.org.uk/Home.aspx

Restorative Justice Council www.restorativejustice.org.uk

Restorative Solutions www.restorativesolutions.org.uk

UNICEF Rights Respecting Schools www.unicef.org.uk/rights-respecting-schools/

6 Lessons from overseas

There are a number of school systems, individual schools and inspirational projects overseas where democratic processes are more embedded than is the case in England and other parts of the UK. In Scandinavian countries, for example, there is an expectation from the outset that parents will share responsibility with schools for their children's education. In Israel, there is a strong democratic movement to promote student voice. In Finland, teachers contribute as a matter of course to their school's development.

Whilst recognising that it is problematic to attempt to import educational practices from one country to another because of differing historical and cultural contexts, it is still the case that we may be able to learn from positive examples elsewhere. This chapter introduces a number of schools, programmes and approaches which foreground voice and participation.

Student voice in Israel - Education Cities

Education Cities is an initiative which links classrooms, schools and regions across Israel and further afield with a view to fostering the healthy development of young people by helping each one to find and express their own uniqueness. This is seen as vital in the development of a healthy society. Their work is based on collaboration at all levels (classroom, school, city, civil society) in order to generate educational innovations which will help to build democracy from the bottom up. Those involved believe that the process of education can best be supported by cities which turn themselves into a fertile ground for learning, places in which all organisations - arts organisations, sports teams, cultural projects and many other enterprises - collaborate in the education of children and young people. "Simply put, a child embraced by the city will reciprocate with love".

Founded by Yaacov Hecht who has been a leading voice in the articulation and development of democratic education since the 1980s, Education Cities has become a powerful force for change. Hecht realised that traditional schools on their own are unable to meet the wide-ranging needs of each and every student.

He proposed that each student develop their own personalised education plan but recognised that this could only be realised by harnessing the resources and support of the town or city where they lived, thereby linking education with employment, urban planning and welfare. Their work currently focuses on the development of innovation labs that bring together teachers and other citizens from the city, and take them on mutual learning journeys.

Hecht established the first democratic school in the town of Hadera back in 1987. At this school every child drew up their own learning programme, stating what and how they would learn, where and when they would learn it and who they would learn it with. The school is publicly funded and has over 500 students, aged 4-18. It is run democratically by students, teachers and parents together. Rules are passed by the school parliament and there are a number of committees which take care of the day-to-day running.

Hadera has influenced many state schools and regional education systems in Israel (and beyond) and there are now around 25 democratic schools across the country. They are based broadly on the ideas of philosophers and educators such as Jean-Jacques Rousseau, Martin Buber and Carl Rogers and hold that children should grow up in an environment in which they can learn the values of democracy in practice and not just in theory. They recognise that education depends on the development of a close, personal bond between teachers and students whereby mutual trust is cultivated and a profound knowledge of the child is generated. Each school operates as a democratic organisation: decision-making takes place through a democratic process which involves the entire school community (students, teachers and parents). As a consequence, learning is dependent on collaboration in order to achieve the goals of the community as a whole.

Building on his early work, Hecht talks about the need for a paradigm shift in education, away from a top-down, pyramid model of schooling towards a networked approach in which every individual is valued and where collaboration across different organisations is key. He sees this shift as instrumental in preparing young people to face the challenges of the world today and in the future.

Changes are required at all levels: in the classroom, in the school, in the city, in the state and globally. Schools must become learning communities in which every student is also a teacher and where learners support each other, working on joint projects. One project called *2021 classroom* encourages educators to reflect on how they develop the space, use the time, create the activities, manage evaluation and collaborate with a wide range of partners in the pursuit of meaningful learning experiences.

The Education Cities approach aims to transform a city into one big school to support the learning of all young people but also as a way of developing the city and changing the lives of adults. Education is no longer confined to taking place within the four walls of a school but becomes a much broader, richer enterprise whereby the development of the individual and the prosperity and well-being of the wider community are inextricably linked. Collaboration between cities leads to the development of nationwide networks of learning and support. This dynamic and far-reaching vision for education and community development is now building in over ten cities and towns across Israel, involving more than 10 per cent of Israeli schoolchildren.

The Ministry of Education has worked with Education Cities in the development of Massive Open Online Courses (MOOCs) to open up exciting and diverse learning opportunities for children and young people. Hecht's work is attracting interest internationally, and educators in a growing number of countries are taking forward these ideas in their own settings.

Emek Hamaayanot – the art of collaboration

Emek Hamaayanot (Hebrew for 'Valley of Springs') in Israel is an *Education Valley* where there is a fascinating collaboration between different sectors of the education community. At its heart stands the joint forum of head teachers, deputy head teachers, the head of the regional council and the head of the regional education department. This group meets on a monthly basis.

Every meeting begins with a participants' circle, which is designed to strengthen relationships and encourage sharing between the different members of the group. The remainder of the session is dedicated to inspiration: at every meeting a different participant is responsible for this part – and for the co-construction of initiatives. Participation in the forum is not mandatory: participants have chosen freely to be part of the group.

Following is a taste of some examples of the group's collaboration:

Head teachers in the valley share with each other the weekly letters they write to their teachers. This initiative helps each head teacher by providing the opportunity to learn from one another.

There is an annual learning day for all teachers in the valley. On this day, the teachers are both teaching and learning. Every teacher is invited to talk about the areas they are passionate about. Each year there are fascinating topics for teachers to explore together. It is a day of dreaming that allows them to disengage from their daily work and to delve into their aspirations whilst engaging in mutual learning and support. At first, only the head teachers took part in this event: now teachers participate as well. The invitation to join in is open to anyone who wishes to do so. Slowly but surely, and with the help of social media, more and more members of staff express their desire to participate.

Project Nesher (Hebrew for 'eagle' and which is an acronym for play-ing, singing and dancing) is an expressive arts project that serves as a meeting platform for various schools. In the past it was, for some, a source of competition and rivalry. Thanks to the collaborative ethos of the *Education Valley*, participants' circles have been introduced at the beginning of every activity and now teachers see the opportunity to build links and share expertise. The circles have generated friendships and a closeness that has brought about joint creative projects and the emergence of professional and social ties between students as well as amongst the staff.

Emek Hamaayanot is successfully leading the implementation of the *Educational Team* model, developed by Education Cities, whereby each class in a school is transformed into a collaborative team with a shared goal and in which all members are both learners and teachers. One of the leading schools in the area was resistant to this approach initially, but through an improvement in relationships and the development of a climate of sharing and support, the school is now leading the way with this work.

A collaboration has started between elementary schoolchildren and pre-school children from a kindergarten which is located inside an archaeologi-cal park. As part of this project the pre-school children teach archaeology to the children from the elementary school. This initiative was born out of one child's dream. With the encouragement of his head teacher, the child brought together a group of children who were interested in archaeology. This group regularly visits the kindergarten to learn from the younger children.

Religious schools and non-religious schools visit one another as part of the work in the valley. Together head teachers have planned and con-structed a professional training programme for their staff.

One of the most recent developments is the so-called *Technological Era*, which is a regional collaborative centre for technological developments, innovative education and employment.

There are many other examples of collaboration and joint work in the valley. Every event or initiative begins with a public appeal to those who are fascinated by a particular topic. This way, people in the valley choose the projects or initiatives in which they would like to participate and our work is thus built on collaboration and networking.

Yaacov Hecht

http://education-cities.com/en/cities/

Class councils in Germany

Today, schools in Germany, as in many other countries, are challenged in terms of how they encourage and prepare students to become active participants in society. In order to support democratic participation, many teachers are looking at how they can develop tangible democratic, cooperative structures within their schools. It is widely thought that this is the best way to counteract dissatisfaction with democratic rules and organisations, xenophobia and right-wing extremism. Research has established a clear link between the experience of democracy and the renunciation of violence. Social change, as well as migration and integration, are changing German society (as well as many other societies around the world) and values, norms and policy are constantly being renegotiated. It is felt therefore that democratic values must be integrated into school life.

Throughout Germany, organisations and initiatives are working to spread the idea of the class council as a means of developing a democratic school culture. The class council is a form of grassroots democracy aimed at encouraging participation. It promotes self-organised learning and responsible and respectful interaction with others and enhances self-efficacy. The fact that Germany has a federalised education structure in which the 16 states each plan their own system makes it easier for different models of schooling to emerge and receive support.

One such pedagogical approach is that of Celestin Freinet (1896–1966), whose ideas inspire educators not just in Germany but around the world, teachers working in early years settings through to university education. Freinet was committed to the concept of productive work and he promoted an active approach to education whereby learning activities bear relation to children's lives in the world beyond school. In class, students construct their own plan of work which they discuss with their teacher. There is an emphasis on working cooperatively and the class meets as a group on a regular basis to coordinate their activities and discuss their work. Children are given space within school to interact in tolerant, considerate, independent and responsible ways and are helped to achieve their own goals. Their joint work is based on respect for children's rights, the rights and interests of others and the advocacy of their own rights.

The class council – aims, structure, process

In Freinet-based learning environments the class council is central to how children work together. Working collaboratively helps children and adolescents acquire cognitive skills and moral competencies in dealing with uncertainties and anxieties as well as developing practical skills. The class council promotes self-esteem, the development of moral judgement and political cooperation. Through the encouragement of collaboration at a deep level it supports cross-cultural understanding. Through their work together children are encouraged to develop constructive ways of dealing with conflict and difficulty, for example through mediation.

Class councils generally have the following arrangements for learning:

- All decisions are made by common consent in the class council. The work of the upcoming week is organised and decided there after the work of the previous week has been discussed and evaluated. What has each student done? How have individual students or groups approached their work? Who is doing what next?
- The class council works through discussion circles. There is a president, secretary, timekeeper and referee, roles which are taken by students in rotation.
- The class council starts with an invitation to report back. Students then talk about new developments. An important element of these discussions is to make room for praise, ideas and criticism.

There are general guidelines for class council discussions:

- The person talking must not be interrupted.
- When it comes to making a decision, everyone – teacher and students alike – has one vote.
- If it comes to important decisions, everybody has to agree.
- Decisions which are made must be respected.
- Timescales that have been agreed must be followed.
- Every student takes on tasks or positions.

The work of the class council can take many different forms. It may include reading texts together, producing the class newspaper, organising different workshops – for example, a creative writing workshop – dealing with school correspondence, keeping the class diary or arranging individual as well as class work schedules. Together students will formulate research questions and make decisions regarding expeditions and projects. The group also takes responsibility for the design and layout of the classroom.

From the outset, children and young people in the class council learn about children's rights as a basis for respectful cooperation. Class councils uphold rights such as participation and equality. They also help with the development of the students' ability to make decisions and to participate in their implementation. In such ways, a Freinet class develops in young people political, moral and ethical judgement and student empowerment. Alongside shaping children's education, it also focuses on how students live together in the community beyond school.

In such ways, the concept of democracy underlying Freinet pedagogy is not limited to the classical interpretation of representative democracy but refers to 'everyday democracy', to values, inclinations and dispositions in daily life. We see democracy not only as a political form but also as a social system and a way of life. Real live democracy means creating a climate of respect, mutual aid and friendliness. Each member of the learning group, whether teacher or student, has the right to be treated respectfully.

Students and educators describe their democratic habits:

"When I listen attentively, I get to know and understand the others better; I learn how others feel and I am no longer an outsider. More openness and trust develops within the class community."

"As a teacher, I have to consider differences and sympathise with the children's and adolescents' feelings and desires. Students and teachers develop a strong sense of justice."

"In our school culture we accept that we are all different. Every human being is unique. There are three rules of behaviour: respect - attentiveness - acceptance".

"I accept each person, female and male, as someone who has the right to have and to express their opinion."

"Teachers and students take on individual and collective responsibility in different areas of school life."

"Teachers cooperate with each other, students cooperate, and teachers and students cooperate."

"Every topic and problem that is brought up will be discussed. Every vote counts the same; everybody gets the right to speak and to express him- or herself."

"Everyone has their own individual freedom within the limits of accepted rules. At school there is tolerance of different nationalities, e.g. of different appearances, different styles of dress."

We see the class council as the heart of democratic school life. Direct democracy is experienced by students on a daily basis and supported by democratic structures at whole school level. Whilst such a democratic whole-school culture exists in relatively few schools across Germany, class councils are integrated into the work of hundreds of schools across the country and many more all round the world with positive outcomes.

Brigitta Kovermann, teacher and researcher, former President of the International Freinet Movement, FIMEM

www.freinet-kooperative.de

www.fimem-freinet.org/en

Teacher autonomy in Finland

Finland is well known for its education system and the fact that Finnish students do well in international comparisons such as the OECD's PISA tests. It does not have a prescriptive national curriculum or a rigid testing and accountability framework and yet it manages to produce results that are the envy of many other countries. What are the secrets of its success? Unlike many other countries, the government does not set out to achieve highly in these tests: their ranking is a by-product rather than a direct consequence of national education goals.

Many attribute Finland's achievements to the quality of its teaching profession. Teachers are held in high regard, they have first-rate training – all, including early years educators, have Masters degrees – and they are trusted to do their job, enjoying a level of professional autonomy that is rare elsewhere. Teaching is thus a highly sought-after profession, entrance to which is extremely competitive.

According to the Finnish educator, Pasi Sahlberg, what makes the difference in Finland is that teachers can "exercise their professional judgement widely and freely in their schools. They control curriculum, student assessment, school improvement and community involvement".

Whilst in many other countries, including England, young people enter the teaching profession with strong intentions to do the best for the children in their care, in Finland teachers actually have the ability and the power to put their ideas into practice. Teachers have thus been instrumental in the transformation of Finland's education system over the past few decades.

What does this mean in terms of the day-to-day practice of teachers in schools?

Firstly, teachers get to plan their own curriculum. They each have responsibility for what happens within their classrooms and are well-equipped for this role. Their in-depth training covers education theory, child development, pedagogical approaches and subject knowledge as well as extensive teaching practice. Teachers are free to try out different approaches in order to best meet the needs of each student in their care. They can be creative in what they do; they can innovate and take risks without fear.

Secondly, teachers are responsible for how their students are assessed in the classroom and can use a variety of methods to evaluate progress and then use the findings to inform next steps. There is only one external general matriculation exam which students sit at the end of upper secondary school. As a consequence of this teachers are not constantly needing to prepare students to jump through hoops, so they have the time and the freedom to teach what and how they think best. The lack of external tests means that teachers themselves are not judged and held to account on the basis of their students' performance. The level of trust that Finnish teachers enjoy from their colleagues, from their communities and from wider society is unparalleled.

Thirdly, teachers spend less time teaching than in many other school systems. Finnish teachers in lower secondary schools teach approximately 600 hours every year compared with the United States where lower secondary school teachers teach almost twice as many hours at 1,080 per annum. (The figure for secondary school teachers in England is only slightly lower than this. Full-time teachers are contracted to work a maximum of 1,265 hours each year of which a minimum of 10 per cent must be given as planning and preparation time.)

As Sahlberg comments in his book, *Finnish Lessons* (2015):

> Interestingly, high-performing nations in all academic domains included in PISA rely less on formal teaching time as a driver of student learning, whereas nations with much lower levels of academic achievement require significantly more formal instruction for their students.

Finnish teachers work as part of a professional learning community and time is allocated during the day for reflection, collaboration, planning and professional development, all of which are crucial to successful professional life. An important part of a teacher's role is pastoral care so time is also available to devote to student welfare and liaising with parents.

These elements together contribute to a shared responsibility and shared accountability for student achievement and well-being within each school. School leaders trust their staff and take account of their views in the development of school policy. In this sense, each school is a collaborative endeavour in which teachers have a voice, where their views are respected and thus inform how the school moves forward.

As Sahlberg acknowledges:

> Learning to teach in a new way is not easy. A safe and supportive professional climate in schools is a necessary condition for professional improvement of teachers. Designing education reforms in a way that will provide teachers with opportunities and incentives to collaborate more will increase the likelihood of sustainable implementation of intended changes.
>
> EUNEC report 2010

The case study below from Kilpinen Comprehensive School is an excellent example of how trust, autonomy and support enable teachers to work together to meet the needs of their students.

Teacher participation and autonomy at Kilpinen Comprehensive School

Kilpinen Comprehensive School is part of the city of Jyväskylä's basic education provision. We have approximately 600 students and 60 members of staff. We take children from grades 1–9, ages 7–16. (Children in Finland start school at the age of seven.) We employ 50 teachers: 6 primary level teachers and 44 subject teachers. In addition, we have a school nurse, school psychologist, secretary, guidance counsellor and several other key faculty members. Three years ago, the local primary school was integrated with our secondary school to form the Kilpinen Comprehensive School.

Leadership

The leadership philosophy of our school is based on the self-determination theory of Ryan and Deci in which the basic needs of an individual – autonomy, competence and community – form the basis of well-being and engagement. These basic needs must be fulfilled in a social context of which the working environment is an excellent example. Professor of Philosophy, Frank Martela, of the University of Helsinki, adds a fourth dimension to the mix: benevolence, which he describes as being good to others. According to Martela, human beings have a natural need to perform acts of kindness towards others who are around them.

Although it is valuable for a superior to support the work of the teachers at the school, shared leadership means that roles and responsibilities are indeed shared. Shared leadership is put to the test in situations when the solution to a problem selected by the working community isn't necessarily the best option. In these cases it is important to remember that there is a need to intervene only in situations where mutual values are being compromised. Otherwise the opportunity for teachers to become authentically innovative in their problem-solving will be compromised. By involving teachers in decision-making, we intend to reinforce the feeling of autonomy and ensure that the goals we have defined as a community permeate everyday school life. As an outcome of open discussions on values and goals we have agreed our school motto, which is '*Learn together*'. Everyone from the faculty participated in this process.

Our working community is quite large, yet communication and shared leadership are things that can be seen in our everyday work. Communication and participation are key. We have an online platform which makes planning, as a community, fairly effortless. The platform is called TACT – Thinking and Creating Together. It can be used for communication purposes, but also as a thinking and planning platform. At the moment it is being trialled and we are developing it as we go along. Already it has been shown to improve collaboration and shared leadership at the school. We have frequent discussions about it and have noticed that those staff members who would normally stand back have been able to voice their ideas and have more of an input. TACT also allows for participation outside school hours. However, the idea is not to replace face-to-face communication but rather to create more versatile opportunities to work together. We reinforce our face-to-face collaboration with short weekly sessions and a longer monthly meeting.

Autonomy and responsibility in the teaching profession

The role of the teacher is changing as the implementation of the new Finnish core curriculum continues. Each education provider has the freedom to develop their own local curriculum based on the core curriculum. They can define the goals for each subject and grade as well as the content that should be taught in support of the learning. Also, conceptions of how we learn, how we assess and how to support the student are outlined. The emphasis is on transferable skills or broad competencies. Teachers have the pedagogical freedom to choose the methods of teaching and assessment as well as learning material. In our school this means that the teachers are extremely aware of the goals of the national curriculum and they work meticulously towards ensuring students receive a fair assessment and outstanding learning opportunities.

Teachers are encouraged to trial a range of pedagogical methods and learn from the experience as well as involve students in the planning, execution and assessment processes. Teachers decide how to divide students into groups in different subjects and can request how their work schedule is planned or ask for additional resources from the principal, e.g. for assistance from the special needs teacher.

The strength of our education system resides in the trust we have in our teachers. We don't control or monitor teachers by standardisation nor do we rank our schools. What is key is for each teacher to be reflective in his or her work. Reflection, feedback and collaboration between teachers is how we maintain teaching quality. The university degree guarantees a firm basis for trust, but of course recruiting the right teachers is also important.

Community and professional development

For the last ten years Kilpinen School has been developing a co-teaching model. In our model, class teachers and subject teachers pair up with special needs teachers. Often the pairs complement each other's subject-specific knowledge or pedagogical skill. In this type of collaboration, responsibility for planning, execution and assessment is shared. Although the main aim for co-teaching is to support student learning, we feel that teachers also benefit from sharing their points of view and they enjoy working together. Due to co-teaching, teachers continue to develop professionally and receive continuous feedback from peers. This model has improved our school's sense of community. We share our passion to make sure the needs of every student are met and that they are able to develop holistically as human beings. We frequently talk about our learning and teaching processes and share materials with one another. Even in difficult situations we know that our colleagues will support us; no one is left alone in their work.

Our school has a 'Developing Schools' team that is responsible for directing our pedagogies. The team works independently, but also with the school board. The role of the team is to plan and organise trialling of learning methods and to support and encourage teachers in their professional development. The team consists of six teachers from different subject areas.

The Developing Schools team has created a way for teachers to take part in a colleague's class, after which they get together to reflect on their experiences. Our teachers were thrilled with this development as they felt it was eye-opening and thought-provoking. We also arrange pedagogical afternoons during which the entire working community gets together to discuss teaching and learning and share experiences and trials. Because of the collaborative and supportive nature of our school community, we now have a sense of excitement for bold experimentation. Teachers continually try out new things in their work – both big and small – and keep learning from their experiences.

Johnny Kotro, Principal and Sari Granroth-Nalkki, Special Educational Needs Teacher and Leader of the Developing Schools Team

Figure 6.1 Happy teachers
Credit: Kilpinen School, Finland

Staff voice in Australian schools

Research in Australian schools shows that, compared to other sectors, schools have some of the highest proportions of engaged staff, with around 80 per cent of teachers passionate about their job, emotionally attached to their school and aligned with its purpose and values. Yet staff involvement tends to be very low, with less than half of teachers reporting that they have an input into decision-making in their schools, or that they are consulted before decisions that affect them are made. Aside from missing out on potentially important and innovative ideas from staff, this is a problem because one of the strongest predictors of staff well-being is the extent to which staff feel involved in school decision-making.

Voice Project

Voice Project is an independent body in Australia with a core purpose to "improve organisations by giving people a voice". They use surveys to improve engagement, leadership and quality, and their fundamental philosophy is that 'voice' generates more information and better decisions, and inspires greater staff ownership and engagement. Voice Project was founded at Macquarie University in Sydney, is made up of a team of workplace psychologists and retains a strong research-practitioner focus.

Since its inception in 2002, Voice Project has worked with many kinds of organisations, across all sectors and industries, including most of the universities in Australia and New Zealand. Whilst they have now also worked with a number of schools, this sector seems to have struggled to establish a 'voice' culture, or to implement effective mechanisms to involve staff in the continual improvement of their schools.

A number of schools have worked with Voice Project and their participation has led to a range of outcomes. One school introduced annual school surveys to inform the school's strategic planning process and to evaluate progress. The principal was new to the school, and was looking for a way to gain input from staff about their experience of working at the school, as well as set a baseline for evaluating strategic initiatives. The input from staff has had a significant effect in shaping priorities for the school in areas such as technology support, professional development and feedback on performance. Staff are encouraged to share ownership of the survey results, and the principal is keen for the survey not to be seen as simply a management tool. He saw seeking feedback through the survey and responding to the results as one way of improving staff involvement. He resolved to be as transparent as possible about the feedback, engaging staff in analysing the results and identifying the way forward. Each year they have trialled

engaging staff through different approaches: conducting debriefs through cross-faculty groups facilitated by a school leader, conducting focus groups on a couple of specific areas facilitated by Voice Project, and a meeting of all their middle leaders.

According to the principal, the open-ended comments in the survey have been particularly helpful in understanding the experience of staff. The school was alerted to a range of issues associated with workflow management that were having a negative impact on well-being, particularly for middle leaders. As a result they focused on workflow changes with and for this group, and achieved significant improvements in workload, work-life balance and flexibility for their middle leaders as a result.

Another school sought the assistance of Voice Project because they also were concerned about the well-being of their staff. After conducting a staff survey, they held a whole staff day where they split into groups to focus on specific issues, unpack the survey feedback in detail and propose possible strategies for improvement. These were captured on the day and reported back to the school executive to further progress.

At a third school, the principal is particularly committed to providing an inclusive learning environment. She has adopted a positive education perspective which operates under the premise that unless students feel safe and secure in their environment, their learning will be compromised. Similarly, unless staff feel supported and valued within the workplace, their performance and productivity will suffer. She was keen to get feedback, using their staff survey, about the extent to which staff felt they were included, respected, affirmed, treated fairly and given equal opportunities. The school is able to evaluate initiatives and track progress over time against comparative data from other schools, which has been helpful in moving forward.

Voice Project say that they are approached by staff after every presentation of results to express gratitude for the opportunity to have a voice. They say that it is often the first chance they have had. Such staff surveys are just one way of involving staff, but have been shown to be effective. School leaders are the key to enabling these opportunities, and to listening and responding to what emerges.

Louise Parkes, Voice Project

www.voiceproject.com

Parental involvement in Estonia

The tiny country of Estonia with its 1.6 million inhabitants is attracting increasing interest in the educational world due to its achievements in the OECD rankings. The results of school students in the 2015 PISA tests are amongst the best in the world. Estonia, which gained independence from the Soviet Union 25 years ago and where 20 per cent of students speak Russian at home, stands out in the international tables for the low number of students with poor skills, for the marginal impact of socio-economic status on students' results and for the high proportion of so-called resilient students (those who perform well despite coming from disadvantaged backgrounds). As such it is a highly equitable school system.

As a rule, children in Estonia must attend the school that is nearest to where they live. In the last 10 years however, parents have become increasingly interested in looking for alternatives: they want to send their children to the school with the best reputation which is usually judged on the basis of results in the state examination at the end of upper secondary school. New private schools have also been established: the number of private school students though still small (5 per cent of all students) has increased by 50 per cent in a decade, whilst the number of school students in general education has dropped by around 20 per cent. However, Estonia considers the comprehensive school – where children study on the basis of a similar curriculum and in similar schools despite their place of residence or the material status of their parents – to be the strength of its school system. One of the goals of the Estonian Lifelong Learning Strategy is to guarantee good-quality basic education close to home for every child and to reassure parents that all schools provide a good education.

Education is valued in Estonian society: teachers are respected and have a significant degree of autonomy within the classroom. It is quite a traditional system with a focus on academic subjects. In recognition of the need to keep pace with its European neighbours, there is growing interest amongst educators in new ideas and approaches and this is opening the door to increased parental involvement. The government-funded project described below illustrates how a partnership between educators, researchers, local officials and parents can play an important role in shifting the ways in which schools work.

Involving parents in school life – the TULUKE project in Tartu

Tartu is the second-largest city in Estonia, with a population of around 100,000. It is the home of the oldest and largest university in Estonia, which was established in 1632. The university and other higher education institutions in the city have approximately 20,000 students. The biggest vocational education centre in Estonia is also located in Tartu. Over 13,000

students attend the 29 basic schools and upper secondary schools in the city. This means that one in every three residents of Tartu is engaged in studying every day.

The schools in Tartu are strong and the fact that the proportion of parents with academic degrees is larger here than in most other regions of Estonia is not the only reason for this.

Tartu is known for its old and unique districts and its active local societies which make sure that this uniqueness is preserved and developed. The City of Tartu encourages its citizens to be active in many ways, for example through participative budgeting which allows citizens to submit projects that contribute to the development of the city and vote for those they support.

This then is the context where a group of parents from two Tartu districts, Karlova and Supilinn, held a meeting three years ago to find out what people knew about the schools in their districts and what more they wanted to know. We came to the conclusion that a municipal school is not an overly open place. People often think that parents only look at state examination results when choosing a school for their children, but we also spoke about enjoyment of school and closeness to home as important criteria. We want our children to be constantly interested in learning, to have the ability to establish and maintain relationships, to never experience bullying and to be tolerant of and open to differences. The list could go on. It goes without saying that a school should provide good academic knowledge and skills. But this is not enough. Children must also be happy and healthy at school. And we became increasingly convinced that parents can help with this.

After these discussions, it was difficult to say 'no' when the Education Department of Tartu City Government invited us to participate in the TULUKE project in 2014, part of which was aimed at developing cooperation between the community and the school. We came up with the following goals for the sub-project of community culture: better information exchange; better representation of interests; and a stronger feeling of community. The Karlova Society and the Supilinn Society participated in the project in addition to four Tartu schools (Forseliuse, Karlova, Kesklinna and Reiniku). Various initiatives ranging in size were carried out in different schools during the project:

1. In 2014, four schools held ideas festivals with more than 200 people. The purpose of the festivals was to highlight the good things that should be maintained and strengthened at schools as well as the things that need improvement. Participants included parents, teachers, students and graduates as well as other institutions in the neighbourhood such as youth centres, nursery schools and neighbouring schools. The

main focus was topics that can be dealt with by schools and communities together.

2. One of the topics raised at the festivals was the limited knowledge of parents and future parents about what actually goes on at schools. This makes it difficult for parents to have a meaningful say in school life. In order to improve this situation, four schools started to organise open days, which give everyone the chance to sit in on lessons.

3. We also worked on making the exciting initiatives of schools more visible by reviewing and developing the schools' websites and organising a competition of videos introducing the schools.

4. The first versions of parent information leaflets were produced in 2016, their purpose being to outline the values and activities of a school and the opportunities of parents to cooperate and get involved.

5. In 2015 and 2016 we conducted a survey amongst the parents of the four TULUKE schools and a few other schools in Tartu. This survey showed, amongst other things, that 60 per cent of parents do not know what the school expects of them in regard to cooperation between home and school. Only 25–50 per cent of parents feel that they can influence different aspects of school life.

6. In order to ensure that the ideas festivals become a tradition and that the ideas they generate are put into action, we thought about ways of involving more parents in school life on a permanent basis from the outset. All schools have a board of trustees according to law, which consists of representatives of the school operator, the staff council, parents, graduates and organisations that support the school. The board of trustees has the right and obligation to have a say on issues concerning the school. Only five to seven parents are usually involved on these boards, and they are unlikely to be able to contribute to many initiatives themselves. And since not all classes are represented on the board of trustees, the connection with all parents inevitably remains weak. In order to get more parents involved, we created boards of parents in the four schools: informal associations of parents that as a rule consist of two parents from each class. In reality, there are more representatives from some classes than others and some, usually classes of older children, have no representatives at all. Depending on the size of the school, the number of members of the board of parents should be 35–70, but there are actually about half as many active participants. However, there have already been some significant achievements in the two years the boards have been operating. Rest areas and exercise opportunities during breaks have been updated; family days and a community day have been organised; seminars have been put on for

parents; and with the support of parents, schools have joined new initiatives such as the anti-bullying programme. At least three more Tartu schools are now establishing boards of parents.

7. In order to strengthen the role of the boards of trustees we also strove to amend the way in which people are elected on to them. As a rule, candidates are nominated by the management of the school. Candidates are usually fairly invisible and so the majority of parents see them for the first time at the school's general meeting at which they have to vote. In order to make the process more open and encourage more voters, one of the schools tested an e-election during the 2015/2016 academic year. Head teacher Kristi Mumm described its impact as follows: "We noticed that parents were happier to run for a place on the board of trustees than before because the new system helped avoid the uncomfortable feeling caused by public voting. It seemed that many of the candidates also gave more thought to the reasons why they wanted to be on the board and consequently wrote more clearly when introducing themselves".

8. One of the outputs of the project was the book *Happy to Go to School: A Manual for Cooperation between Home and School* (2016) which is based on experience gained during the project, good practice in cooperation between homes and schools in Estonia and abroad, and scientific research. The book is available online free of charge and the experience of the TULUKE project has thus been shared in schools, at parent meetings, at seminars, at conferences and at other events with more than a hundred schools to date.

It is too early to speak of the long-term impact of the project on schools and children, but we have got the ball rolling. To quote one of the authors of *Happy to Go to School*, Kersti Kaljulaid, who is the current President of the Republic of Estonia, "the cultural changes in this direction which have already begun require us to find great examples to encourage others and to figure out how to help create the new normal. This is how we will secure good education and also soften the edges of the school system".

Although the project officially ended in spring 2016, the activities have only now started to gather momentum. Boards of parents are operating in the majority of schools for the second year and a meeting in early 2017 proved that despite the difficulties, nobody is ready to throw in the towel. This means that the time is right to boost the involvement of parents in school life.

Kairit Peekman, Department of Education, Tartu City Government and leader of the TULUKE project and Aune Valk, parent and promoter of school-community cooperation in a TULUKE project school

Figure 6.2 Ideas Festival
Credit: TULUKE Project, Estonia

Parental participation in the Netherlands

Parental involvement in education in the Netherlands is underpinned by the freedom of parents to choose a school for their child. The vast majority of schools are independently run but fully funded by the state, with the effect that there is a wide variety of schools, with state-funded alternative schools such as Steiner, Montessori and Jenaplan schools existing alongside more traditional schools. Parents in the Netherlands have responsibility for the care and education of their children and it is expected that they will choose a school which reflects their values at home. Schools fall into one of four main categories – Catholic, Protestant, public (each representing between 25 and 32 per cent of pupils) and non-denominational (representing 5 per cent). Parents also have the right to establish their own schools for which they can receive funding, although nowadays this is more difficult to secure than it used to be. A number of Muslim schools have been established, particularly in urban areas, by parents who felt that their values were not reflected in the local schools. Because parents have this freedom to choose a school, there is an expectation that they will therefore be generally committed to and supportive of the school's policies and practices. There is also an expectation on schools that they will work in partnership with parents.

Schools are seen as belonging to parents, and the school boards which run schools exist to serve their interests. Parents tend to be well represented on the board and also on the 'participation council', a body which consists of parents and teachers and through which parents can influence decisions taken by the school board. All schools also have a parents' council. This body exists as a forum on which parents can discuss a wide range of issues to do with bringing up children as well as educational matters. Through this body they can make suggestions to the participation council and the school board as well as raising issues concerning the day-to-day running of the school with the school management.

Parents commonly support school life in all the traditional ways, by assisting with school trips and social activities, helping children negotiate the traffic outside school and by carrying out repairs to school buildings. Parental involvement in the education process itself has grown to the extent that many schools now have parents helping out in the classroom. It is recognised by some schools that involving parents, with their diverse knowledge and skills, enables them to offer a broader curriculum to their students. But at the same time, because of the increase in the number of women working, the amount of help that is offered has reduced.

In recent years schools have been given increased autonomy, taking over some of the functions that were previously carried out by government authorities. Schools now have more freedom to design their own programmes and curriculum and evaluate their activities. This means that they are able to define their own goals and assess the extent to which they are achieving these goals. Government inspections are about overseeing the effectiveness of this process rather than checking to see whether the school is delivering a government-imposed agenda. This degree of autonomy brings with it considerable scope for parents – through the parents' council, the participation council and the school board – to determine school policy. In practice, the extent to which this happens depends largely on the attitude of the school management to parental participation.

There is recognition that for parents to be able to contribute effectively to school policymaking they need to develop the necessary skills to fulfil such a role. There is a national parents' organisation and its main function is to represent the voice of parents to the government and to advise parents as to how they can work with their child's school. Responsibility for education policy is highly devolved and central government is concerned mainly with financing the system, controlling standards through the school leaving examination and maintaining provision. There is growing concern amongst educators however that the government is increasingly influenced by the Anglo-American pre-occupation with testing and league tables and that this is being reflected in education policy and in the inspection framework.

Structures are in place at national and at school level to support parental involvement in education and participation in decision-making. As in all countries and all schools, the degree to which parents are involved on the ground depends on the views and willingness of individual teachers to collaborate with parents. It is against this backdrop that CPS, one of the main advisory organisations for schools in the Netherlands, is working to support greater parental collaboration in education through its work on *Parent Involvement 3.0*.

Parent Involvement 3.0 - a framework for home-school cooperation

In the Netherlands, parental involvement in school life is taken very seriously. There is an awareness that for students to flourish it is essential that there is good collaboration between the school and the child's parents. A lot of Dutch schools are now working with the concept *Parent Involvement 3.0*. It is an approach which helps school to achieve a constructive collaboration. At the outset there is a discussion about what parental involvement means, and then we outline examples of how our approach works in practice.

Parent Involvement 3.0
Information that flows from the school in a one-sided way rarely leads to an increase in parent involvement. In contemporary society, where every day we are inundated with information, there is a limit to what we can take in. On the other hand, with the increased use of social media, people are more and more used to interaction, speed and efficiency in communication. Despite this, many schools continue to send information home in the traditional manner, using newsletters and email. A lot of information reaches parents quickly but in a way that doesn't allow for interaction. This is called Parent Involvement 1.0. There is no real contact. Consequently, parents can sometimes react strongly and may send emotionally charged responses. Parent Involvement 2.0 is a step up from this in that it enables parents to respond but there is still no direct communication. There is a gap between parents' and teachers' worlds and it is all too easy for schools to see parents as a nuisance when they make contact. Parents often experience teachers as dismissive and feel uninvolved with the school because they are not partners in the process of supporting their child's learning. By way of contrast, Parent Involvement 3.0 is the version of communication that is necessary to take interaction between schools and parents to a better level by ensuring that there is a genuine dialogue.

In summary:

- Parent Involvement 1.0: The school sends information out to parents. This is one-sided communication where the school decides the timing, the format and the content of the information.

- Parent Involvement 2.0: The school sends information to parents and allows parents the opportunity to send information back. But there is still no direct communication: the information is just a collection of one-way messages that does not necessarily lead to collaboration.
- Parent Involvement 3.0: The school and parents share and search for new information with a common goal in mind for both parties – the healthy development of the child, that is, the student.

But why should schools (or parents) make the switch to Parent Involvement 3.0? It is because it improves student outcomes. Research studies clearly show children do better when their parents and teachers work together in finding what's best for them. It helps students to feel better about their learning. It can also help with preventing absenteeism and possibly bullying.

This approach also helps in doing things more efficiently. It can save time, and also energy, for both teachers and parents. Parent Involvement 3.0 is a way of thinking. When every teacher and parent consistently acts according to this way of thinking, it increases mutual understanding and it enables teachers and parents to help each other, support each other, motivate each other and inspire each other – with the student's best interests in mind.

Parent Involvement 3.0 is reached by letting go of all existing approaches to parental involvement. And the recipe for implementation has four essential ingredients:

1. A startup meeting at the beginning of every school year for the parents, student and teacher or tutor to meet together.

2. Individual arrangement of meetings: school, parents and students agree on the type and frequency of communication based on the developmental needs of the student.

3. A reception or event at the beginning of the school year for parents and children in one class so they will get to know each other (again), thereby enabling relationships to be built at the start of the new school year.

4. The assignment of buddy or mentor parents so that parents can support each other when they have problems, for example with language or with their child's development.

By consistently using these four ingredients, Parent Involvement 3.0 can become a reality with positive benefits for children, for parents and for the school.

Here are three examples of schools that use this approach.

Coffee XL at Onze Wereld

Onze Wereld ('Our World') is a primary school with approximately 850 students in The Hague. Students come from more than 30 different cultures. Three times a week the school puts on coffee for parents at the start of the day in the school theatre. At every meeting there are between 50 and 80 parents. They drink coffee and talk together and then at 8.45 the principal or a guest speaker joins in to talk about issues which are of interest to them. These short workshops of 15 minutes or so ensure that parents are an essential part of the development of the school and the colourful community of Our World. (www.onzewereld.net)

Education with parents at De Bussel

At De Bussel ('The Bundle') Primary School in the village of Vlijmen, teachers and parents work closely together. Parents come into school regularly to support their own children. This makes it possible for children to have individual support; parents become their personal mentor. Teachers focus on observing and coaching. Regularly they lead a session with the student and the mentor-parent. They decide what to aim for and how to reach the student's goals. In this way parents and teachers co-create education for subjects like maths, spelling and reading skills, and students of all different levels benefit.

Children who participate together with their parents have a more effective education. Data shows that their results can be improved by 30 per cent. It also has a positive impact on their well-being and this impacts positively on home life and learning. These days at De Bussel it is common for students and their parents to work together in this way and the school community is increasingly proud of this cooperation.

Startup meetings at Roemer Visscher College

At Roemer Visscher College in The Hague, teachers hold startup meetings with parents at the beginning of each academic year. Maths teacher Nurtin Aydin reports that:

> After the startup meetings parents become more involved in the education and career paths of their children. This might result in some students changing their subject choices having discussed options with their parents and teacher. Parents often start to do their own research with and for their children to help them make the best decision. Because of this collaborative process a significant number of students change direction but as teachers, we feel that this helps them make better choices.

Joris Spekle, Senior Adviser and teacher and Peter de Vries, Principal Adviser, author, trainer and parent

Lessons to learn?

Notwithstanding earlier comments about the difficulty of transferring practice from one country to another, are there any generic lessons that can be learned here in the UK from these and other examples from overseas?

First, as far as student voice is concerned, the Education Cities project and the Israeli democratic schools highlight the importance of more personalised approaches to learning. Children are all different and with such widely varying needs that it makes sense for every child to have their own education programme. In an information-rich, ICT-connected, highly mobile society it is not beyond the bounds of possibility to personalise learning in this way. What is interesting about the Israeli work is the recognition that educating the next generation is the responsibility of towns and cities, not just of schools and parents. This calls to mind the African proverb "it takes a village to raise a child". The Israeli example shows a way to collapse the boundaries between school and community so as to draw on the many untapped skills and resources that exist in every locality which could help to expand the horizons and extend the experiences of young people.

It is impossible for schools on their own to hold all the skills and information that will be needed by children and young people growing up in contemporary society. With ever-shrinking budgets, the pressures on schools and on teachers within the traditional model are growing inexorably. How much more attainable is an approach to education which identifies the strengths and needs of each individual child and which leads to an individual learning programme that supports his or her development by harnessing the contribution of parents, family members and other individuals and organisations within the community. Not every child needs the same input at the same time and a one-size-fits-all school system is hugely wasteful of resources. A more personalised approach puts the child at the centre of the learning process as an active participant in his or her education rather than a passive consumer of a blanket, catch-all curriculum. Such an approach is far more likely to lead to a genuine engagement with learning. Whilst the Israeli focus is on student voice and participation, at root this is about developing a more collaborative approach to education which does not rely solely on teachers and schools.

This chimes with the project in Tartu in Estonia where parents are being asked for their views about education and invited to contribute to the development of their schools in order to create schools that children are happy to go to: schools which parents are happy to send them to. In many places parents' views are neglected and yet they bring a crucially important perspective. They hear what their children say about school and as a consequence have a useful view about what works and what needs to change. It is interesting that the president of Estonia recognises the key role that parents and others outside the school can play in the transformation to a system with 'softer edges'. In the Netherlands, where parents have long had a voice in education decision-making, it is recognised, however, that democratic engagement is not enough. The project being led by CPS to develop *Education 3.0* is about building a genuinely collaborative relationship between home and school so that parents and teachers can work together to support the child. The child is at the centre of a relationship which seeks to foster a shared responsibility for educational progress and well-being.

What then is the role of the teacher in all of this? Rather than being a deliverer of information and administrator of tests, the Finnish system indicates that the role is more as a mentor, guide and coach. Teachers have responsibility for the holistic development of their students, they oversee their academic progress as well as their pastoral care and have time to collaborate with colleagues and with parents in order to provide the best possible support and challenge. They are valued, they are trusted and they are respected to do this job. It is a highly skilled role, requiring lengthy and in-depth training and practice: not just the cursory year that is standard practice in England. Those countries which cut corners with their teacher education programmes are unlikely to get the best outcomes for their young people.

What comes through in these varied examples is the importance of collaboration, the centrality of relationships and the need, not just for the different parties to have a voice, but to be genuinely listened to by others so that together they can find the best way forward for the school and for each child. It is not about student voice, or parent voice or teacher voice: it is about developing a school community which is open, which listens and which finds a way forward based on a shared understanding and a common vision. No blueprints, no end points – just a democratic process that helps to make schools into dynamic learning environments, best able to meet the needs of the community they exist to serve.

The next and final chapter will draw attention to a range of resources and processes that can be used to help schools on their journey towards building such a shared vision and a common sense of purpose.

Bibliography

Butrymowicz, S. (2016) Is Estonia the new Finland? *The Atlantic Magazine*, www.theatlantic. com/education/archive/2016/06/is-estonia-the-new-finland/488351/

Department for Education (DfE) (2016) *School Teachers' Pay and Conditions Document*. London: Department for Education.

Hecht, Y. (2011) *Democratic Education: Beginning of a Story*. New York: AERO.

Martela, F. (2012) *The Four Elements of Motivation*, published online at: http://frankmartela. fi/2012/07/the-four-ultimate-elements-of-motivation-how-to-get-the-best-out-of-you-and-others-and-how-robots-will-save-the-world/

Ryan, R. M. and Deci, E. L. (2000) Self-determination Theory and the Facilitation of Intrinsic Motivation, Social Development, and Well-being. *American Psychologist*, 55(1): 68–78.

Sahlberg, P. (2015) *Finnish Lessons*. New York: Teachers College Press.

Websites

Education Cities http://education-cities.com/en/cities/
European Network of Education Councils www.eunec.eu/
   Report on *Participation and Stakeholder Involvement in Education Policy Making*
   available at: www.eunec.eu/sites/www.eunec.eu/files/event/attachments/report_
   brussels.pdf
Finnish National Agency for Education www.oph.fi/english/education_system/teacher_
   education
Hadera Democratic School, Israel www.democratics.org.il/site/index.asp?depart_id=125189&
   lat=en
Hundred https://hundred.org/en
Institute for Democratic Education Israel www.democratic.co.il/en/ide/
International Freinet Movement www.fimem-freinet.org/en

7 Strategies and resources to support transformational change

So far the book has looked at a variety of schools which are listening to the voices of their teachers, students and parents. If those voices are to lead to positive and sustainable change, schools need to have strategies and approaches that are embedded into their ways of working to ensure that teachers, parents and students are consulted in a meaningful and ongoing way and that their views are taken account of in whole school decision-making.

This chapter gives examples of some approaches, resources and frameworks which are being used in different settings to support transformative change:

- The contributions from the International Futures Forum and Education Scotland both exemplify approaches to whole school transformation that involve all the key stakeholders.
- The overviews of the Learning Leader programme and the Self Managed Learning model are examples of student voice approaches which show ways of involving students in decisions about their learning, contributing to class-wide, departmental and whole school improvement and at individual level.
- The resource on parent councils gives an introduction to how schools can listen and respond to parents' views in the development of school policy. The Parent and Community Skills Audit is a resource that schools can use to help collapse the boundaries between school and community to the benefit of both.
- Information provided by the Education Survey and Research Service gives an overview of how the Keele Surveys can be used to identify issues to address within a school and which can inform a change process. It includes a sample of the kind of data and feedback provided to schools following the completion of their surveys.
- Finally, the Campaign for Education in Brighton and Hove is an example of local action aiming to express democratically the voices of parents, teachers, students and local people in shaping local education provision.

Change Approach 1

Transformative innovation in schools

The International Futures Forum (IFF) is working to support transformative innovation in schools and has designed an approach and a set of resources to facilitate the change process. The following is an overview of the framework.

Throughout the developed world, school systems face the same challenge, according to Karl Fisch in his blog The Fischbowl – to prepare students for "jobs that don't yet exist, using technologies that have not been invented, in order to solve problems we don't even know are problems yet". Yet no school system in the world, as far as the IFF knows, has adequately addressed this challenge, even though all of them know they must do so.

Incremental innovation, making our existing systems work better, is necessary but not sufficient. We also need *transformative innovation* – innovations that start at a small scale but have the capacity over time to shift the entire system and deliver outcomes the existing system cannot even imagine.

Working closely with schools and other partners, the IFF has developed a straightforward approach that encourages such transformative innovation. The approach gives professional staff, school leaders, local government officials, parents and, importantly, learners the tools, prompts and frameworks to think beyond normal constraints and the support to move towards their radical aspirations.

The practical approach developed is described in detail in the book *Transformative Innovation in Education* and more generically in *Transformative Innovation: A Guide to Practice and Policy*. Schools work through a change process using a *Three Horizons Kit* that provides all the materials to open up an informed and challenging conversation about the future which then feeds into a far-sighted plan to transition towards the organisation's aspirations over time.

The plan will include a portfolio of transformative initiatives and intentions. Those ready to pursue these are then supported by a set of change management tools that enable the move from insight to action. The result is a down-to-earth, practical agenda that combines improvements for the present with future-facing innovation. It is a strategy to 'redesign the plane whilst flying it'.

The approach has yielded impressive results across a range of schools in widely different contexts and at different stages of development. It is now being adopted in different countries including Australia and the United States.

The Kit

The *Three Horizons Kit* for schools is designed to enable school leaders to facilitate a wide-ranging and strategic conversation about the present and the future.

The first stage is a conversation about the current operating landscape of the school, informed by a set of prompt cards containing known trends written as short

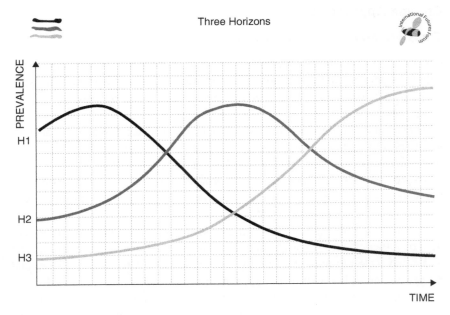

Figure 7.1 The Three Horizons Framework
Credit: International Futures Forum

statements about the changing world, changing education policy and practice and changing young people. Users record the outcomes of their conversation on 'post-it' notes on the Three Horizons Chart (see Figure 7.1). The chart outlines the Three Horizons using the two axes of prevalence (how dominant something is in the culture) and time (how that dominance is waning over time and giving way to new practices).

With the addition of a die, a timer to regulate play if necessary and a simple set of instructions to read and communicate to the other 'players', any group leader can manage a strategic conversation that, in a couple of hours, helps the team to describe in more detail an extended view of their operating landscape. This extended view will cover current concerns, promising innovative actions and aspirations for the future. The process is very straightforward. Senior students with experience of the *Three Horizons Kit* have themselves subsequently led teachers through such a process.

The second stage involves interpreting the landscape that is revealed – and, through refinement and prioritisation, incorporating the insights from that strategic conversation into a school improvement plan. This provides an innovation portfolio consisting of three kinds of action:

- Sustaining innovations required to address concerns about the existing system in order to keep it running.

- Decommissioning aspects of the existing system that have no place in the ideal future.
- Transformative innovations that will pave the way towards the future vision.

The Kit has been designed and developed for primary and secondary schools. There is also a version specially modified for use in higher education settings.

Self-evaluation

A critical first step in navigating towards a desirable future, or indeed towards any point, is to determine your starting position. School improvement and transformation methods therefore all set great store by self-evaluation.

With this in mind, the IFF have developed a simple cloud-based software package that allows schools to evaluate themselves and identify factors impacting effectiveness and performance around nine key areas whilst highlighting the relationships between them. The key areas are: outcomes, learning and teaching, improvement, leadership, engagement of staff, ethos, strategic relationships, resources and external factors.

The tools

The *Three Horizons Kit* will allow any school, or any group, to have a well-informed, challenging and far-sighted conversation about the present and the ways that things may unfold into the future. The Kit is intuitive and game-like and has been designed to be self-facilitated with all the instructions and support required.

Moving from the insights of the Three Horizons conversation into the domain of improvement planning involves a more disciplined process. The Kit includes a Phase 2 process for translating the initial strategic conversation into the broad outlines of an improvement and innovation plan.

Thereafter, making headway requires individuals to absorb the implications arising from the strategic conversation, and to be courageous in taking the first steps into the unknown towards their envisaged 'third horizon'. Equally, individuals need to do so with discipline and a plan that is rooted in the challenges of the real world.

A set of powerful tools has been designed to help take this work forwards and these tools have been incorporated into the IFF approach. Their use depends on a certain level of skill and understanding – and so the full set of tools is only available at present as part of a package of training from one of the IFF's recognised facilitators. However, it is possible to achieve a good practical knowledge of the two central tools for work in education – *Impacto* and *Implemento* – by reading *Transformative Innovation: A Guide to Practice and Policy* and the downloads which are available via the IFF website.

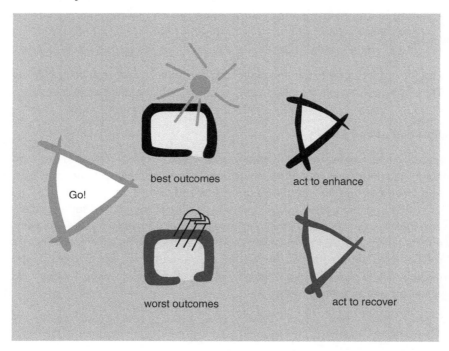

Figure 7.2 Implemento* – a framework for considering potentially risky change
Credit: Executive Arts Ltd

The book *Transformative Innovation in Education* also has advice for those designing national policy frameworks: a six-point plan for incorporating transformative innovation into any change strategy.

*The image of *Implemento* is copyright © 1989–2016 Executive Arts Limited and redrawn with the copyright holder's permission.

The *Transformative Innovation in Education*, the *Transformative Innovation* books and the *Three Horizons Kit* are available from the International Futures Forum. Further information about this approach and resources to download are available at:

www.iffpraxis.com

Change Approach 2

Transforming learning

Education Scotland has designed a Transforming Learning framework to support transformational change in Scottish schools as well as in early learning and childcare settings, community learning and development, further education and at local authority level.

The Transforming Learning approach has been developed by Education Scotland, the national educational improvement agency in Scotland, with a view to empowering transformational change in the Scottish education system. It is based around a *Three Wheels Framework* which encourages practitioners to agree the actions needed in their setting to bring about transformational change and then follow them through to successful completion over a period of one to three years. Whilst this approach was developed with a focus on Scottish education priorities, the approach is transferrable to other situations.

Practitioners are encouraged first of all to work in teams to complete a *Scoping and Scanning* cycle to reflect in detail on:

- What they need to stop doing
- Exemplars and top priorities for their school or setting
- What they want to do but can't do yet
- The barriers
- Solutions to the barriers
- Possibilities for the future

Participants are asked to respond to these six prompts to enable them to understand the past, present and potential future in their learning environment, taking account of the needs and contributions of all the different stakeholders (learners, teachers, parents, employers etc.). It is suggested that they reflect on practical, technological, social and political considerations.

The process continues with a cycle of looking inwards, looking outwards and looking forwards:

- Looking inwards: to evaluate performance at every level within their setting and use the information gathered to decide on what needs to be done to improve.
- Looking outwards: to learn from research, from others and from best practice and use this to facilitate innovation and creativity and to inform improvement actions.
- Looking forwards: to explore what the future might bring and use this information to anticipate what change is required to ensure the education system is responsive to the future needs of all learners.

Evidence, evaluation frameworks, research information and resources can all be recorded on an *Inwards Outwards Forwards Wheel*. Once this exercise is completed, the team should use this knowledge to consider what the top priorities are for their school or setting in terms of future transformational actions to be undertaken so as to be responsive to the future needs of all learners.

The team then needs to agree and define their chosen actions in detail and link them to their institution's improvement plan, defining the Why, What and How for each action: *Why* do they need to do it; *What* it will achieve and *How* it will be undertaken. This information can be recorded on a *What Why How Change Wheel*. Once the detail is recorded for each of the proposed transformational actions, the team should go back round these three questions for a second time to calibrate or check their responses and adapt them as appropriate to ensure that they are clear and coherent. The chosen actions should then be recorded on a planning sheet so that they are visible to staff, parents and students.

The number of actions agreed will depend on the size of the school or setting. In a small institution or team one action may be sufficient, rising to up to eight for a larger setting. For each action, any risks need to be considered in terms of whether they are manageable or are to be avoided. It will then be important to consider what the identifiable outcomes and tangible results will be for learners and how the evidence and likely impact can be recorded.

This whole cycle of self-evaluation and planning is designed to support transformational change and leadership at all levels within the education system.

Education Scotland has produced a number of resources to support this change process and a short film to explain how it works in practice. Further information is available on the National Improvement Hub at:

https://education.gov.scot/improvement/Pages/cre27transforminglearning.aspx

Change Approach 3

Learning Leaders

The Learning Leaders approach enables young people to have input into decisions about their learning and to feedback to teachers, school departments and school leaders about their lessons. This is an overview of the training programme which is run within a school to foster the skills that enable students to perform this role effectively.

This training programme has been developed with the aim of encouraging and supporting students to take a more active role in their learning and to work collaboratively with teachers to enhance learning and teaching. It is about giving students a voice and ensuring that they have a say in their own learning, as well as being able to support teachers in the classroom and represent the views of their peers in discussions about learning at departmental and whole school levels. Students who undertake such a role benefit from training to ensure that they can be as effective as possible.

The programme is divided into seven separate training sessions teaching students how to:

- Plan and lead parts of a lesson
- Construct and deliver plenaries and starters
- Support weaker students

- Observe lessons and give constructive feedback to teachers
- Contribute to discussions about learning and teaching at class level, at departmental and at whole school levels

Getting started

The Learning Leaders programme is dependent on the support of teachers. A good starting point is therefore to identify a small number of teachers who would like to participate in the programme. It is also crucial to have committed students taking part. The programme is suitable for mixed-ability students: enthusiasm and a desire to improve learning are requirements for participation. Students generally apply to become a Learning Leader by completing an application form which includes a reference from one of their teachers. All interested students are interviewed and then selected by the staff who have agreed to develop the programme.

The training programme is based on 14 hours of teaching alongside various extended learning tasks for students to complete outside of the sessions. Schools can adapt the programme to suit their own circumstances, using just some of the sessions if they prefer. However, students who complete the whole programme will be better equipped to act as Learning Leaders.

To support the training, all of the students are issued with a notebook for use as a reflective journal in which they can record how they have worked as a Learning Leader as well as their own feedback. Keeping such a journal is a requirement for completing the Learning Leader training.

Each session is two hours long; however, the programme can be adapted to suit different school timetables. For example, it can be arranged as a weekly lesson for the duration of a term. At the end of each session, a task relating to the content of that session is set so that the students have the opportunity to put into practice what they have learned. Below is the outline of the training programme.

Learning Leader training programme outline

Training session 1:
Understanding Teaching and Learning

- Introduction to the programme
- Getting to know each other exercises
- What is a Learning Leader?
- Structure of lessons: What makes a good lesson and what makes a good teacher?
- Vision and values – overview of the school

Task to complete before the next session:
Before the next session, using what you know about Learning Leaders already, act as a Learning Leader once and write about it in your journal and ask a member of staff to sign.

Training session 2:
Understanding Teaching and Learning continued

- What are learning objectives and why are they important?
- How do students learn?
- Looking at different ways of learning
- How do we know we are learning?

Task to complete before the next session:
Pick one of your lessons and review the learning approach used and write about this in your reflective journal.

Training session 3:
Leading in lessons

- What does it mean to lead in a lesson?
- Designing and leading starters and plenaries
- Assisting teachers
- Supporting other students

Task to complete before the next session:
Ask one of your teachers if you can design and lead a final plenary session for one of their lessons. Once you have completed this task, ask the teacher for feedback about how you got on and record this in your journal.

Training session 4:
Communication skills and team building

- What are communication skills?
- Written communication – letters and reports
- Oral communication – presentations, speeches
- Visual communication – body language
- Listening
- Practical team building tasks

Task to complete before next session:
Write about a time when you have used good communications skills and when you have used good teamwork skills and reflect on these examples.

Training session 5:
Observing lessons and giving feedback to staff

- How to observe a lesson – what to look for
- Agreeing an area of focus with the teacher
- How to record observations
- Giving appropriate feedback to the teacher

Task to complete before next session:
Arrange with a member of staff to observe a lesson; agree the area of focus and give appropriate feedback. Write about this in your journal and get the member of staff to sign.

Training session 6:
Leadership skills

- What makes a good leader?
- Types of leadership
- Developing leadership skills

Task to complete before next session:
Lead an activity – it can be within your school or outside. Reflect on how you did, the skills needed and your performance as a leader.

Training session 7:
Review of sessions and skills developed

- What makes a good Learning Leader?
- Being a good role model and gaining staff and student trust
- Review of previous sessions: What skills have been developed?
- Checking Learning Leader reflective journals
- Agreeing next steps

What next?

There are multiple ways that Learning Leaders can be deployed across a school. They are generally each assigned to a department and it is up to the department to decide how best to deploy them. Designated staff within each department are encouraged to meet regularly with their Learning Leaders to agree tasks, discuss feedback and agree ways forwards. To ensure that Learning Leaders are deployed on a regular basis across the school, a range of measures are recommended:

- Setting termly tasks for the Learning Leaders
- Running CPD for teachers to ensure their awareness of the Learning Leaders and how they could be deployed (this session can be led by the Learning Leaders themselves)
- Involving Learning Leaders in staff recruitment
- Using Learning Leaders as ambassadors for the school
- Incorporating a section on Learning Leaders into forms for lesson observation and lesson planning
- Hosting a Learning Leader celebration event to acknowledge the students' hard work

Further information regarding the Learning Leaders programme is available from Alternatives in Education www.alternativesineducation.org

Change Approach 4

Self Managed Learning

Self Managed Learning is an approach to learning in which school-aged students have a say about what, where and how they learn and where and whom they learn it with. This approach is used at the Self Managed Learning College as well as with groups in schools across the country.

Self Managed Learning was developed in the late 1970s, drawing on different personalised approaches such as action learning and independent study, with the aim of enhancing their most useful aspects whilst guarding against anything which tended to constrain learning. The elements of a Self Managed Learning programme are explained below, along with how the programme works in practice.

There are two levels of learning involved in a Self Managed Learning programme. The most obvious of these is that students choose learning goals and pursue those goals over the period of time of the programme. Those learning goals will be as varied and as individual as the students themselves. The less obvious level of learning is that, in the process of identifying and pursuing their learning goals as part of a learning group, students will be developing as active learners. They will be increasing their capacity to actively pursue their own learning both independently and interdependently.

Programme in brief

The Self Managed Learning approach has two main elements at its core: the learning agreement and the learning group. These bring focus and coherence to each individual's learning activities. Identifying learning goals (and writing them up in the learning agreement) helps to focus attention on what one wants to learn and what one needs to do to learn it. Additionally, the learning agreement provides a way to pull all the learning together in terms of an individual's aims. The learning group provides a structure through which an individual can keep track of their progress with their learning goals.

The learning agreement

Each member of a learning group produces a learning agreement, a document laying out what and how they want to learn. It provides a guide to each student's intentions. Their learning goals are explored in relation to five questions (see below). Consequently, the learning agreement is equivalent to that individual student's curriculum for the duration of the programme. The advantage in having this in written form is that it can be returned to when taking stock of progress, when planning next steps and, additionally, it provides a basis for resource planning.

During the development of the learning agreement, students will discuss their thoughts within their learning group, and other learning group members may be able to help them clarify their intentions. In effect, it becomes an agreement between the individual student, who is agreeing to pursue those learning goals, and the learning group, who collectively agree to support that student in the learning they need to do to accomplish their goals.

The learning agreement is created by writing down the answers to five questions in relation to the student's goals:

1. Where have I been?
2. Where am I now?
3. Where do I want to get to?
4. How will I get there?
5. How will I know I have arrived?

The final question incorporates how the students themselves will know they have accomplished their goals but also how others within the school will recognise the outcomes of their learning.

The learning group

Each student will be in a learning group of up to six students, together with a learning group adviser. Attending the learning group meetings is a commitment of the programme. The learning group functions as a supportive, stable base for a peer group of learners of a similar age. It is within the learning group that each student's learning agreement is discussed, refined and agreed. The learning group also provides a supportive structure over the period that learning goals are being pursued.

During learning group meetings, each student is given a period of time within which to explore the learning activities they have undertaken, what has been learned from these activities and to talk through any problems that have come up along the way. They can also think through their next steps towards the learning goal. Each individual has the opportunity to decide how to best use their time slot in the meeting. During a given student's time slot, the other members of the group may have questions or comments to put forward with the aim of assisting that student's learning. From the learning group meeting, the students launch out into the school and wider community where the activities in pursuit of their goals are undertaken.

Learning group advisers

The role of a learning group adviser is somewhat like a mentor (and quite unlike a teacher or tutor). Their main responsibility in the learning group is to keep its focus on learning. They 'hold' the structure and ensure that each student has an individual time slot to address their own learning. Peer group support and challenge is very valuable, and it requires students to listen to and understand one another. The learning group adviser's special role is to assist the students to help each other and to this end, much of the time they operate like other learning group members: asking questions, offering things for a student to consider, helping the student think through next steps, etc.

Running a Self Managed Learning programme within a school setting

Schools vary as to how they start a Self Managed Learning process. Students will need support in working in new ways. Teachers may have been used to a classroom-based approach and it can seem strange for them too to work in a different way.

Introduction processes vary and need to respond to the context of the school. A typical process is to have a meeting with each student and, depending on the age of the student, their parents. The main aim is for the learning group adviser to talk to the student about the programme and its aims. If parents are present, they are able to ask questions and get any clarification needed.

Students need to know they will be engaging in a somewhat different learning experience than they are used to. They will need precise information. Even with documented materials students often struggle to understand how things will work and it can take time to make the changes.

At the beginning of a programme, learning groups will form and meet their learning group adviser to talk through the purpose of the group, how meetings are structured, what they will be doing during the meetings and how often they will meet as a group. They will also discuss what ground rules they are going to work to as a group. The learning group adviser will explain how they will go about developing a learning agreement, explaining how to use the five questions format. Learning groups generally meet once a week.

At the first learning group meeting, students will address question 1 of the five questions which are used as a framework for the learning agreement. This helps the group to get to know one another. The learning group adviser begins the process by talking through their own past experiences, most particularly their educational experiences.

Meetings of the learning group follow a common structure. The essential elements in the learning group meeting process are:

- Check in: This provides a brief opportunity for students to share their pre-occupations.
- Agenda setting: This establishes what needs to be covered during the meeting.
- Individual time slots: These are the essence of the meeting. During the individual's time slot they are in control and decide how they want to use the time. It is an opportunity to have five or six people focus exclusively on what they choose to bring to the meeting. Questions the learning group adviser might use include the following:
  - What do you want from your time?
  - What have you learned from your time?
  - What will you do next?
  - What will you do for the next group meeting?
- Process review: This is an opportunity to review how they are working together as a learning group.
- Check out: This is a quick round of responses to the meeting.

Assessment

Although there is no formal examination and no qualification involved, there can be value in undertaking an assessment at the end of the programme. Part of being an effective learner is being able to evaluate what you have done. The assessment process can help in developing that ability.

The other learning group members, including the learning group adviser, can question the student and also give their own thoughts (in effect, their assessment of the student's own assessment). It can be useful for the student to hear how their activities have been viewed by others.

Ian Cunningham - From the Self Managed Learning College Staff Handbook. Further information, training and resources on Self Managed Learning are available from the Self Managed Learning College.
http://college.selfmanagedlearning.org/

Change Approach 5

Setting up a parent council

The following resource supports schools and parents in setting up a parent council to help listen and respond to parents' views, especially with regard to school decision-making. It is taken from a document entitled *Developing Parent Voice at your School*, produced by PTA UK and Parent Councils UK.

Many schools work hard to engage parents recognising that children do better when their parents are involved in their education. And many parents would like to have more of a say in school decision-making but are not sure about the best way to go about making their voice heard. Most of the decisions made by schools affect parents one way or another and so it is only right that they should be able to contribute their views. Those schools which do involve parents in decision-making have generally found that it helps to develop a positive partnership between home and school and that this ultimately benefits the children.

PTA UK and Parent Councils UK are both committed to building parent participation so that schools can best meet the needs of their communities. Ofsted expects schools to listen and respond to parents' views and looks for evidence of this when they carry out an inspection. They believe that it strengthens the school to have procedures for parents to be consulted. Inspectors in Scotland, Wales and Northern Ireland also look for evidence of parental engagement.

What is a parent council?

Parent councils enable parents to contribute to school decision-making on issues which affect them. Depending on the size of the school, parents in each class, tutor group or year group nominate a parent or a number of parents to represent them. Alternatively, parents can volunteer to join the parent council. The parent council meets on a regular basis (usually termly) to discuss issues put forward by parents or by the school. The council has an advisory and a consultative role in that it can advise the school leadership and governing body of the views of parents on different issues, and it can consult parents on behalf of the governing body or school leadership.

Table 7.1 Suggested topics for consultation with parents

Some issues on which parents can usefully contribute:

Homework	School trips
Behaviour and discipline	Parent donations
Lessons and learning	Break/lunchtime activities and
Curriculum and assessment	arrangements
Reports and parents' evenings	Healthy food
Health and safety	School grounds
Transition	Wraparound childcare
Conversion to an academy and which MAT	Uniform
(Multi Academy Trust) to join	Links with the community
School policies such as admissions	Parent volunteers
Environmental sustainability	Personal, social, health education

The participation of the head teacher (or other senior leader) and a governor is crucial so that they hear what parents have to say and can take account of their views when they are making decisions.

The following flow chart illustrates the recommended steps to be taken in setting up a parent council.

Head teacher, governing body, parent or teacher suggests setting up a parent council

**Working party established to discuss way forwards
(to include parents, governor(s) and a senior member of staff)**

Consultation carried out to find out views of parents, governors and staff about how the parent council could best work

Working party to discuss outcomes of consultation

First meeting arranged involving head or senior leader – publicised to all parents and staff

First meeting held to discuss how best to organise body, positions of responsibility, timing and venue, forthcoming agendas

Outcomes of meeting reported back to governing body, school leadership, staff and parents

Future meetings arranged to address issues raised by parents

Before coming to a decision about the best way to proceed it is advisable to consult widely so as to enlist the support of as many people as possible. In order to be inclusive it is important to make sure that a range of parents are involved so that different viewpoints are heard and discussed.

The parent council will need to think about how best to establish effective two-way communication with the wider parent body to ensure that parents know how they can contribute their views. Different forms of communication can be used: for example, online surveys, a web-based forum, suggestion box in reception, text messaging or emails.

Suggested agenda for first meeting

1. Introduction - explanation of why a parent council is being set up
2. Description of how the parent council might work
3. Discussion in small groups of issues that parents might want to have a say in
4. Feedback from the above discussion
5. Suggestions for next steps

Membership

In setting up a parent council you will need to think about how it will be organised. Will you have a parent representative from each class or will you have several representatives from each year group? This will depend to an extent on the size of the school.

There are a number of options as to how this is done:

- Parents are nominated by other parents.
- Parent representatives are invited by staff.
- Parents can put themselves forward. If the number of volunteers exceeds the agreed number for the committee or council, a decision will have to be taken as to how best to proceed and whether an election is needed.

Roles

The parent council may want to appoint people to specific roles such as chair, vice chair and secretary. In choosing people for these roles it is important that they have the necessary skills. At the beginning a member of the school staff or governing body may need to work alongside parents or offer support or training to parents to help them develop the skills needed to be effective.

Keeping the momentum going

Once the parent council is established, thought needs to be given to how to keep moving forward by:

- Making it enjoyable so that people want to participate
- Having some quick wins so parents see that they can make a difference
- Finding different ways to listen to parents
- Bringing in new members
- Letting staff and parents know about current issues under discussion
- Publicising successes

Formalising the parent council

Once a parent council is established, a next step is to agree terms of reference or draw up a constitution in order to formalise the work of the group. This will include information such as:

- Name of the group
- Aims and objectives
- Membership
- Key roles
- Meetings (to include details of the annual meeting)

Links with other groups within the school

The parent council will be most successful if it connects with other key groups within the school. The link with the governing body is crucial as it is through this link that parents' views can be reflected in school decision-making. There may be an existing group of engaged parents, such as a PTA: if so, it will make sense to connect with this group. It will be valuable to maintain contact with staff as it is helpful for staff to know what the current issues of concern are for parents and vice versa. By linking with the student council, students and parents may be able to work on issues together. Links can be made by sending representatives to each other's meetings or through the sharing of notes from meetings. Developing these links helps to build up a common sense of purpose between parents, students and school staff by sharing concerns and addressing challenges together.

This is an excerpt from Developing Parent Voice at Your School available at: www.pta.org.uk/Parents/Get-involved-at-school/Developing-parent-voice-at-your-school

Further information available from PTA UK www.pta.org.uk

Change Approach 6

Parent/Community Skills Audit

The Parent/Community Skills Audit is a simple survey that can be used to begin the conversation about how a school can become better integrated with its community by sharing skills and resources.

On its own, a Parent/Community Skills Audit does not represent a strategy for transformational change, but given that few schools currently invite the involvement of parents and members of the local community in a systematic way, such a survey can be the starting point for developing this partnership as a precursor to deep-rooted change and a cultural shift. Schools which have used such an audit have reported significant benefits in terms of increased support for the school within the wider community.

An example of such an audit is included below.

Parent/Community Skills Audit

Do you have any skills, life experiences or interests which you would be prepared to share with our students and our school? If so, we would love to hear from you. We are keen to build links between the school and our local community. As the African proverb says – "It takes a village to raise a child".

Ways in which you might contribute to the school could include:

- Giving a talk about your work
- Assisting with a class project
- Helping a child read
- Volunteering in class
- Running a workshop for our students
- Talking to a class on a subject of interest
- Visiting during our special curriculum weeks
- Running or helping with an after-school club
- Offering work experience to a student
- Organising a visit to your workplace
- Sharing your skills – e.g. gardening, ICT, graphic design, painting and decorating

Ways in which the school might be able to help you:

- Offering a room for a meeting (for a nominal fee to cover our costs)
- Use of our facilities in the evening (e.g. sports facilities, computers)
- Opportunity to do an English, maths or ICT qualification

If you are interested in any of these, please contact the School Office.

Please complete the form below and return it to the school office or email to: [insert school email address]

Name:

Child's/Grandchild's name (if applicable):

Preferred method of contact (email/phone number):

Job, skills, life experiences or personal interests (please give details of what you could offer):

Workplace involvement
Would you or someone from your workplace be able to give a talk to our students or welcome a group of students on a visit to your place of work? Could you offer expertise? Would you consider sponsoring an area at the school? Can you offer a work placement to one of our students for one or two weeks?

Community involvement
Are you involved in a community group that might be able to work with us? If so, please let us know about it.

Can you give an indication of how often you would be able to help and how much time you are able to offer? (Please circle as appropriate)

- Once a week
- Once a month
- Once a year
- One day   Half a day   Two hours
- Other – Please specify

Are any days of the week more convenient? If so, please specify:

Thank you for your time. Someone from the school will be in contact with you shortly.

Change Approach 7

Keele Surveys

The Keele Surveys provide data to schools in response to surveys of teachers, support staff, students, parents and governors. The information which is gathered offers a useful starting point for schools wishing to take account of the views of key stakeholders in moving forwards.

Now operated by the Education Survey & Research Service (EdSRS), the survey service at the University of Keele has over 25 years' experience of providing objective research and evaluation support to schools and education authorities using a range of attitudinal surveys. These independent surveys provide detailed impartial analyses of the views of pupils, parents, teachers, support staff and governors about the quality of various aspects of school provision (both in response to tick-box questions and through the opportunity for free-text comments). They are widely used by schools in the process of self-evaluation and review in order to develop effective improvement strategies.

The Keele Surveys can be undertaken at any time during the school year. The questionnaires are available in paper format or online and are completed anonymously. Once a school has commissioned a survey, the materials (or bespoke link if being undertaken online) and full instructions are sent within 24 hours. The completed questionnaires are then returned to EdSRS for analysis. Where the surveys are being conducted online, schools are sent regular updates on completion rates.

In the case of the pupil questionnaire, the broad areas of school life in which questions are grouped are as follows:

- The level of satisfaction with the school experience (e.g. Are you usually happy at school?)
- The quality of pupil/teacher relationships (e.g. Do the teachers really listen to what you have to say?)
- The perceived extent of parental support for pupil learning (e.g. Do your parents help and advise you with your schoolwork?)
- The influence of the peer group (e.g. Do other pupils make fun of people who work hard?)
- The level of pupils' commitment to learning (e.g. Do you work as hard as you can in school?)
- Pupil well-being (e.g. Do you agree that this school encourages pupils to adopt healthier lifestyles?)

The parent questionnaire covers the following broad areas which impact upon the quality of the child's experience:

- The school and its standards
- Communication between school and parents

- The relationships between parents and teachers
- The quality of children's experience in school
- The effectiveness of the teachers
- The well-being of their child

The teacher, support staff and governor questionnaires cover broad areas such as:

- The quality of the school
- The pupils
- General classroom practice
- Professional development and support
- Leadership and management

Participating schools receive both a hard copy and an electronic copy of each survey report from EdSRS. All survey reports include tables comparing current findings with previous Keele Survey findings at the school (where available) and with extensive national averages. In addition, all survey reports include an executive summary to facilitate dissemination of key findings to stakeholders.

An example of a 'mock up' executive summary is shown below:

PUPIL SURVEY OF SCHOOL LIFE

Brig House School

Executive summary

Satisfaction with the school experience

- 90% of pupils think Brig House School is a good school
- 92% agree that the school is giving them a good education
- 70% think that the school rules are fair and reasonable
- 94% say that they are happy there
- 74% think that most things they work on in school are interesting

Relationship with teachers

- At Brig House, 57% of pupils believe that most teachers are respected by pupils
- 80% think they get on well with the majority of their teachers
- 82% say they enjoy most of the teaching
- 90% agree that most of the teachers encourage them to work hard
- 82% say that teachers take the time to explain things

Parental support for pupil learning

- 80% of pupils say their parents/carers ask about what they are learning at school
- 85% say that their parents/carers help and advise them with school work
- 96% say their parents/carers attend parents' evenings/review days to discuss their progress

Peer group influence

- At Brig House, 33% of pupils agree that pupils encourage each other in lessons
- 76% of pupils agree they enjoy working in groups with other pupils
- 78% of pupils say that other pupils rarely or never make their life miserable

Pupil commitment to learning

- 91% of those questioned at Brig House suggest that their work is important to them
- 65% say they get so interested in their work that they don't want to stop
- 81% say they usually work as hard as they can

Pupil well-being

- 61% of pupils agree that Brig House encourages them to adopt healthier lifestyles
- 88% of pupils say that they usually feel safe at school
- 77% agree that the school is helping them to set realistic targets for academic improvement
- 65% agree that Brig House encourages pupils to develop self-confidence and make the most of their abilities

Comparative data

In the pupil survey report, the school's figure for each question is compared to the average percentage of responses received to the relevant question from Keele EdSRS pupil surveys conducted nationally. Additional information for the report is obtained by analysing groups of questions together in order to identify attitudinal differences in respect of the following six areas:

pupil satisfaction, relationship with teachers, parental support, peer group influence, pupil commitment to learning, and pupil well-being. This technique allows for a broad-brush approach to interpreting the data, which facilitates comparison between schools.

The chart in Figure 7.3 summarises Brig House's overall figure for each of the six categories, together with the EdSRS national database average (based on responses from 40,000 pupils in the UK):

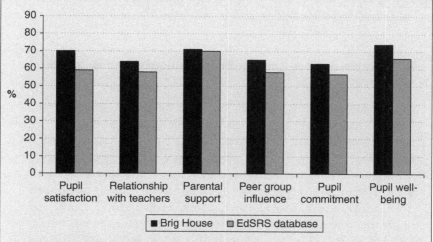

Figure 7.3 Sample chart showing feedback from pupil survey
Credit: EdSRS

The pupil survey also provides comparisons with previous Keele EdSRS pupil surveys carried out at Brig House. Table 7.2 compares the category figures from this year's survey at Brig House with those from the previous survey undertaken at the school:

Table 7.2 Pupil feedback data

Brig House	2015-16	2016-17
Pupil satisfaction	69%	70%
Relationship with teachers	63%	64%
Parental support	73%	71%
Peer group influence	64%	65%
Pupil commitment	62%	63%
Pupil well-being	72%	74%

Further details about the Keele surveys are available on the EdSRS website at www.edsrs.org.uk.

Change Approach 8

A Campaign for Education

A local education campaign can bring together teachers, parents, governors and the general public to express the democratic community voice with a view to helping to shape local education provision.

Information about the campaign that has been established in Brighton and Hove, taken from their website, is included below. It shows how such a campaign can work and the kinds of issues it might address.

Why do we need a Campaign for Education in Brighton and Hove?

Education is under attack. We see this in the pressure of targets in the curriculum, in attempts to turn schools into academies without consultation of parents, staff and local people, and in severe cuts, financial chaos and privatisation in the further, higher and adult education sectors. But these are just symptoms of an ongoing process of transformation of education which prioritises employability and seeks to apply the discipline of the market.

For students, it means more standardised testing (even for early years), rote learning, larger classes, an increasingly polarised and fragmented education system and fees for further and higher education which are higher than many places in Europe.

For teachers, it means more top-down prescription of how to teach, worsening of pay and conditions of employment and unreliable judgements of performance and a devaluing of their professional expertise.

For parents and the wider community, it means a less planned, more divided school system with some schools significantly better resourced and benefitting from more freedoms than others and increasing hidden costs of education (for instance, expensive uniforms and technology).

As part of this process, the influence of large commercial organisations is growing. They sponsor academy chains, run the governing bodies and influence the curriculum and how it is taught. They are not answerable locally and have no obligation to meet the needs of all young people. They are already finding ways of making financial gains from the state education system paid for by taxation.

We support the call for a National Campaign for Education. Locally we want to work to build alliances between all those working in education and their unions, children, students and parents, and with other related campaigns (e.g. the Charter for Primary Education, the Campaign for State Education, the Campaign for the Public University and the Too Much Too Soon Campaign) to fight for education as a public good rather than a business opportunity.

Locally, we want to provide a focus and a forum for debate and activity in campaigning for an education system that is:

- Inclusive, and designed to meet the needs of all, from early years to adult avoiding damaging notions of fixed ability and associated labelling.
- Planned and managed, through local collaboration rather than competition and in the widest public interest.
- Democratically accountable to communities, students and staff through (for instance) elected representatives and open meetings.
- Publicly funded and providing a high-quality equitable service, free at the point of delivery.
- Delivered by trained and qualified staff, with professional autonomy over curricula and assessment and working in the interests of learners.

We are committed to working with anyone who shares these ideas and values and to support local campaigns which share these aims.

Further details about the Brighton and Hove Campaign for Education are available at:

https://campaignforeducation.wordpress.com

Conclusion

Each of the examples included in this chapter offers a way for schools and education settings to build the participation of their key partners or stakeholders so as to become more open, transparent and democratic. Whilst all the examples are quite different in their scale and focus, each approach has led to a significant cultural shift in institutions where they have been adopted. They demonstrate that there is no one-size-fits-all solution to educational change and that different strategies and approaches suit different settings. I leave the final word to the International Futures Forum:

Incremental innovation, making our existing systems work better, is necessary but not sufficient. We also need 'transformative innovation' – innovations that start at a small scale but have the capacity over time to shift the entire system.

For information

Alternatives in Education www.alternativesineducation.org

The Campaign for Education in Brighton and Hove https://campaignforeducation.word-press.com/

Education Scotland https://education.gov.scot/

Education Survey & Research Service www.edsrs.org.uk/

Executive Arts www.executivearts.co.uk

Fisch, K. *The Fischbowl*. http://thefischbowl.blogspot.co.uk/

International Futures Forum www.internationalfuturesforum.com/

PTA UK www.pta.org.uk/

Self Managed Learning College http://college.selfmanagedlearning.org/

Looking ahead

The aim of this book has been to explore how teachers, students and parents can have more of a say in the education system: in how schools are organised and in what and how children learn. It has not been about promoting a specific view of education; rather, it has explored the processes: the means by which educational purposes and approaches can be conceived, agreed and enacted democratically – a precursor for a democratic society. It has been written as a response to the enormous changes that have taken place over the past 30 years, changes which have resulted in an increasingly centralised system where the voices of those who teach, those who learn and those whose children go to school have become marginalised. There is widespread concern amongst educators, academics and parents that these changes are not in the best interests of children.

As has been observed in preceding chapters, all maintained schools are subject to a rigid national testing framework; local authority responsibility for and oversight of education has all but disappeared and power is now concentrated in the hands of the Secretary of State for Education. The introduction of academies and free schools has led to a fragmentation of the educational landscape and a transfer of control to the unelected chief executives of academy chains. In some chains, individual governing bodies have been abolished and replaced with an overarching governance structure, thereby reducing the possibility that school communities can influence decision-making in their own setting. Democratic accountability for education has thus been decimated at national, local and school level. This is troubling, not just because of the impact on schools but also because of the wider effect on society.

It has already been noted that these changes relate only to the English system. In Scotland, Wales and Northern Ireland, accountability continues to be exercised through local authority and school governance structures. In a recent article comparing the four education systems, Professor Tim Brighouse, former London Schools Commissioner, suggested that:

England remains the poor relation with its centralised system and weakened local government. If a sense of powerlessness is the enemy of democracy, England is more at risk than the other three countries.

The Scottish and Welsh systems are undergoing radical reform, a process which, in both countries, involves strengthening the teaching profession and encouraging new ideas to build the active participation of parents and children. By contrast, in England, there are only isolated examples of inspiring practice in schools where head teachers are prepared to challenge the system and do things differently. What is needed here too is an educational framework which celebrates innovation, which unleashes the creativity of teachers, students and parents and where exciting ideas can blossom and take root. What might such a framework look like?

At school level

We need to listen attentively to the voices of teachers, parents and young people, hear what they are saying and bring those voices together into a strong and powerful school community voice. Young people often have a clear sense of what helps them to learn; teachers as professionals know how best to support their students, and parents have much to offer in terms of helping their own children and the school. Furthermore, schools will be strengthened by reaching out to their local communities, involving local people - with a diversity of skills and talents - and local organisations in the education of the young. Schools on their own cannot offer the breadth of experiences and opportunities that constitute a rounded education. We must broaden the focus of education and life-long learning to include communities. Professor Stephen Ball (Ball 2013) of University College London argues that:

> We need to reconnect education to democracy and work towards a relationship between schools and their communities. We should recognise the centrality of education to larger projects of democracy and community building. This is about communities, parents and students having a say in deciding what, how and by whom they are taught - and whether, how and when they are tested, among other things.

At local level

In each area, a local education panel or forum could bring together the voices of different key groups to help shape local provision. These panels would address fundamental questions about the wider purposes of education and how these could be provided for across the region. Local businesses, environmental organisations and arts and sports bodies would have much to contribute to local planning to ensure a holistic offer. Professor Richard Hatcher of Birmingham City University sees the need for:

> a local Education Panel with representatives from schools, parents and the local authority who would develop a long-term strategic plan for education. Membership of the Panel would also include representatives of governors, teachers, school students and community representatives.

At national level

It is vitally important that key partners and stakeholders are consulted about education policy at national level. At the moment we do not have national representative bodies for teachers, students or parents. Michael Bassey, Emeritus Professor at Nottingham Trent University, calls for:

> A national education council, comprising teachers, MPs, academics and other prominent members of society [to] collate evidence of what [is] happening in schools, commission research, organise nationwide sampling of basic skills and report to parliament... Parliament's deliberations would be discussed by every school governing body. A Secretary of State for Education would be unnecessary. One junior minister would suffice.

By passing responsibility for the development of national education policy to such a council, it would end the political football that education has become whereby new policies are introduced with every change of government. This is about taking education out of the hands of the politicians and trusting a body of experts and key stakeholders to make decisions that are in the interests of children and of society – unconnected with the policy agenda of any political party.

A number of European countries have education councils which perform such a function and which are consulted on a regular basis by their governments and provide advice about education policy. These councils, which may be regional or national, bring together policymakers, stakeholders and experts in a transparent consultation process and are based on the recognition that stakeholder engagement and participation leads to better policymaking because it connects policy decisions with action on the ground. Education councils work differently in different countries and are seen to play a major role as an interface between regional, national and international policies. The European Network of Education Councils (EUNEC) has members in Belgium, the Czech Republic, Estonia, France, Greece, Ireland and the Netherlands amongst others. Its work is funded by the European Commission to strengthen participative processes and share good practice to assist with implementation of the strategic framework for European cooperation in education and training. Whilst acknowledging that the UK is on its way out of the European Union and membership of this organisation may not therefore be open, its work to support the existence of education councils in encouraging and supporting stakeholder involvement in decision-making is certainly something that the Department for Education could learn from.

> Participation and consultation of citizens and stakeholders is a key element in policy decision-making. It is generally being recognised as a main indicator of good governance.
>
> Brans, M., Van Damm, J. and Gaskell, J.

Looking at the wider social picture and how education fits into it, the environmental commentator, George Monbiot, has argued that we need to rebuild local communities in order to overcome the isolation and alienation that many people feel. By developing a richly participatory culture we can remake society at grassroots level and in so doing "it will eventually force parties and governments to fall into line with what people want".

Schools are a good place to start and could be the hub of each community, a catalyst for the development of shared values based on cooperation and community regeneration. Michael Fielding, Emeritus Professor at the Institute of Education in London, has written extensively about the need for 'person-centred' educational approaches and argues that we must:

> reclaim education as a democratic project and a community responsibility – and the school as a public space of encounter for all citizens.

It is hoped that this book has provided some ideas, resources and practical strategies that will enable schools to listen to all of their stakeholders so that they can best meet the needs of young people in contemporary society and help them to create a positive future. By working together in our own communities, we can challenge the democratic deficit and rebuild our schools from the bottom up. It can be done.

Bibliography

Ball, S. (2007) *Education plc: Understanding Private Sector Participation in Public Sector Education*. London: Routledge.

Ball, S. (2013) Free schools: Our education system has been dismembered in pursuit of choice, *The Guardian*, 23 October 2013. Available at: www.theguardian.com/commentisfree/2013/oct/23/education-system-dismembered-choice

Bassey, M. (2015) *Charter for Educational Advance*, published at www.free-school-from-government-control.com

Brans, M., Van Damm, J. and Gaskell, J. (2010) *Education Councils in Europe: Balancing Expertise, Societal Input and Political Control in the Production of Policy Advice*. Brussels: EUNEC. Available at: www.eunec.eu/sites/www.eunec.eu/files/attachment/files/rapport_volledig.pdf

Brighouse, T (2017) How can we tackle hate crime with four school systems? *The Guardian*, 27 February 2017. Available at: www.theguardian.com/education/2017/feb/28/hate-crime-school-british-values-tim-brighouse

Carnie, F. (2017) *Alternative Approaches to Education: A Guide for Teachers and Parents*. London: Routledge.

Fielding, M. and Moss, P. (2011) *Radical Education and the Common School: A Democratic Alternative*. London: Routledge.

Hatcher, R. and Jones, K. (2015) For an Empowered, Democratised and Properly Resourced Local School System. *Stand Up for Education*. London: NUT. Available at: www.teachers. org.uk/files/reclaimingschools-essays-9963.pdf

Monbiot, G. (2017) *All Together Now*. Available at: www.monbiot.com/2017/02/09/all-together-now/

Wilby, P. (2016) Parents out, chief executives in: Our schools will be anything but free, *The Guardian*, 21 March 2016. Available at: www.theguardian.com/commentisfree/2016/mar/21/schools-academies-democracy-educational-standards-accountability

ABBREVIATIONS

ATL	Association of Teachers and Lecturers
CPD	Continuing Professional Development
DCSF	Department for Children, Schools and Families
DfE	Department for Education
DfES	Department for Education and Skills
EdSRS	Education Survey & Research Service
EFC	Excellent Futures Curriculum
ESRC	Economic and Social Research Council
GCSE	General Certificate of Secondary Education
GERM	Global Education Reform Movement
HGIOS	How Good Is Our School
ICT	Information and Communications Technology
MAT	Multi Academy Trust
MOOC	Massive Open Online Course
NUT	National Union of Teachers
OECD	Organisation for Economic Cooperation and Development
Ofsted	Office for Standards in Education
OM	Opening Minds
PISA	Programme for International Student Assessment
PSHE	Personal Social and Health Education
PTA	Parent Teacher Association
RRSA	Rights Respecting Schools Award
RSA	Royal Society for the encouragement of Arts, Manufactures and Commerce
SAT	Standard Attainment Test
SEN	Special Educational Needs
SENCO	Special Educational Needs Coordinator
SMSC	Spiritual, Moral, Social and Cultural Development
UNCRC	United Nations Convention on the Rights of the Child

CONTRIBUTORS

Katie Alden – Stanley Park High School, Sutton, London
Anna Bolt – Glyncollen Primary School, Swansea, Wales
Ros Brown – Independent Researcher
Wendy Cameron – Antonine Primary School, Glasgow, Scotland
Campie Parent Council – Campie Primary School, Musselburgh, Scotland
Ian Cunningham – Self Managed Learning College, Brighton
Thomas Darling – Beckfoot School, Bradford
Alex Denham – Beckfoot School, Bradford
Peter de Vries – CPS, the Netherlands
Michael Fielding – Institute of Education, University College London
Lauren Flynn – Integrated College Dungannon Student Council, N Ireland
Layla Funnell – Horndean Technology College, Hampshire
Sharon Gibson – Devonshire Infant Academy, Smethwick, W Midlands
Aaron Graham – Integrated College Dungannon Student Council, N Ireland
Sari Granroth-Nalkki – Kilpinen Comprehensive School, Finland
Frances Green – Loreto Grammar School, Cheshire
Gill Halls – Beckfoot School, Bradford
Sam Harding – Bedales School, Hampshire
Ed Hawkings – Sweyne Park School, Essex
Andrea Hazeldine – formerly of Uckfield Community College, East Sussex
Yaacov Hecht – Education Cities, Israel
Arnas Irzikevicius – Integrated College Dungannon Student Council, N Ireland
Clare Jarmy – Bedales School, Hampshire
Coral Joseph – Quintin Kynaston School, St John's Wood, London
Russell King – Passmores Academy, Essex
Perpetua Kirby – Independent Researcher
Johnny Kotro – Kilpinen Comprehensive School, Finland
Brigitta Kovermann – Researcher and Teacher, Germany
Graham Leicester – International Futures Forum
Teresa Little – St Paul's RC Academy, Dundee, Scotland

Katie Lobb - Mayflower Community Academy, Plymouth
Alasdair Macdonald - Morpeth School, Bethnal Green, London
Kenny McKeown - Dundee City Council, Scotland
Louise Parkes - Voice Project, Sydney, Australia
Kairit Peekman - Department of Education, Tartu City Government, Estonia
Susan Piers Mantell - Learn to Lead, Wells, Somerset
Jemima Reilly - Morpeth School, Bethnal Green, London
Joris Spekle - CPS, the Netherlands
Martyn Steiner - formerly of Oxford Montessori Schools
Hayden Taylor - Unloc, Portsmouth
Aune Valk - TULUKE School Project, Estonia
Fred Williams - Burlington Junior School, New Malden, London

Also by Fiona Carnie:

ALTERNATIVE APPROACHES TO EDUCATION:

A GUIDE FOR TEACHERS AND PARENTS

SECOND EDITION

Alternative Approaches to Education provides parents and teachers with information and guidance on different education options in the UK and further afield. This new and expanded edition, including additional chapters and up-to-date contact details, explains the values, philosophies and methods of a range of alternative approaches available outside and within the state system, as well as if you're 'doing it yourself'.

Illustrated throughout with the first-hand experiences of children, teachers and parents, it provides lists of useful contacts, sources of further information and answers to common questions. Together with brand new chapters on recent research and contemporary debates, and on Free Schools, it covers:

- Small alternative schools
- Steiner Waldorf education
- Democratic schools
- Alternatives in the state system
- Parents as change agents
- Setting up a Small School or Learning Centre
- Home-based education
- Flexible schooling

Exploring why alternative approaches to education are needed, this accessible and informative book challenges the dominant educational orthodoxies by putting children first. It will be of interest to teachers looking to build on their knowledge of different educational approaches in order to find new ways of working. It is also an ideal introduction for parents deciding how best to educate their children.

2017 | Routledge | 256pp
PB: 9781138692084 | HB: 9781138692060 | EB: 9781315533216

INDEX

Note: illustrations are indicated by *italicised* page numbers and tables by **bold**.